MICHAEL BENTINE is perhaps best known as a founder member of 'The Goon Show' and a successful star of radio and television, but in recent years he has devoted more and more time to writing. His books on the paranormal, *The Door Marked Summer* and *Doors of the Mind*, were both bestsellers.

OPEN YOUR MIND
THE QUEST FOR CREATIVE THINKING
Michael Bentine

CORGI BOOKS

OPEN YOUR MIND: THE QUEST FOR CREATIVE THINKING
A CORGI BOOK 0 552 13492 9

Originally published in Great Britain by
Bantam Press a division of Transworld Publishers Ltd

PRINTING HISTORY
Bantam Press edition published 1990
Corgi edition published 1991

This book is set in 10/11 pt Times

Corgi Books are published by Transworld Publishers Ltd., 61–63
Uxbridge Road, Ealing, London W5 5SA, in Australia by Transworld
Publishers (Australia) Pty. Ltd., 15–23 Helles Avenue, Moorebank,
NSW 2170, and in New Zealand by Transworld Publishers (N.Z.) Ltd.,
Cnr. Moselle and Waipareira Avenues, Henderson, Auckland.

Made and printed in Great Britain by
BPCC Hazell Books
Aylesbury, Bucks, England
Member of BPCC Ltd.

To Frances Barbara Forbes ('Nursie') whose love, loyalty, wisdom and laughter enriched the lives of everyone fortunate enough to know her.

CONTENTS

Contents

AUTHOR'S NOTE

'Open your mind to receive inspiration. Trust your intuition, always filtering your thoughts through rational thinking . . . and you won't go far wrong.'
Adam Bentin (1886-1963)

That excellent advice, given to me by my father, helped me to open a door to Inner Space, the domain of the unconscious mind. Through that portal, in my imagination, I have passed safely many times into other, wonderful worlds: the boundless realms of creative thought.

Although I cannot claim that this book will help those with little or no imagination, I believe that it will give readers, who possess the basic ability to conjure up pictures or images, concepts, symbols, sounds, or music in their minds, further opportunities to extend their personal frontiers of creative imagination.

That is what my own unusual experiences and the small store of knowledge that I gained from them, have done for me.

I also believe that we are entering a New Age, in which the open-minded will inherit the earth.

PREFACE

I cannot presume that every reader of this book will be acquainted with my previous ones on the subject of my experiences of the paranormal titled *The Door Marked Summer* and *Doors of the Mind*.

Therefore, I hope that those of you who are familiar with these books will bear with me, if you recognize brief statements about certain stages of my life, as this book contains an updated reassessment of these unusual experiences.

Apart from that, the rest of this book is new and is, in the main, about the process of creative thinking, and the best methods, as taught to me by my father, for developing and controlling the imagination.

It also contains startling and revealing material about some of the powerful influences that can manipulate our minds, and through them, our lives.

Many people have no idea of the extent of these psychic pressures. For this reason, I hope to pass on to my readers some of the effective techniques of psychic self-defence, which I have learned from my own experience.

I am convinced that, in our present chaotic world, anyone with an open mind has the best chance of survival.

INTRODUCTION

Creative and Destructive Thinking

This book is mainly about the extraordinary powers of the mind and how we can release this inner force, through the development of our creative imagination.

I discuss the areas of creativity in which I have been involved, including my fifty years of research into what is loosely described as the paranormal, the art of healing and the power of positive thinking, for in the light of my own experience, this has been and still is the most important factor in my survival as an artist, a writer, and an open-minded person.

However, this book is also about the terrifying destructive power that the mind can generate, if it is *misused*.

Of course, a rational, open mind can differentiate immediately between these extremes of the application of human will, even in the shadowy area of the world of politics, where one often merges with the other, in the name of pragmatism. But a closed mind, such as that of a fanatic or bigot, cannot tell which is which.

Therefore, I must make certain points clear:

Nothing can be created by hate.

Negative forces can only destroy.

Consequently, before anyone attempts to open his or her mind to the extraordinary latent power contained therein, my advice is: First of all, you must get rid of greed, envy, jealousy, and hate, and choose instead someone you admire who you can use as a yardstick for your creative development and mental growth.

For example, when I started working as a comedian and scriptwriter, I modelled my visual comedy on the outstanding examples of the great comedians of the silent screen. These, in order of personal preference, were Buster Keaton, Charlie Chaplin, Laurel and Hardy, Harry Langdon and Harold Lloyd.

All these delightful and creative performers had brightened my childhood with the originality and professionalism of their comedy, and even today, whole sequences of their silent movies still remain as fresh in my memory as the moment I first saw them and I am just one of many millions who continue to enjoy them.

When I started to write books I was influenced by authors such as Rudyard Kipling, Conan Doyle, John Buchan, Ernest Hemingway and a number of others, whose work had enlivened my imagination during my early life.

Although I have never consciously copied the style of these creative writers and performers, their work served me well as an inspiration.

Whether the reader of this book thinks pictorially, audio-visually, multi-dimensionally, mathematically, metaphysically, symbolically, or in the mode of pure concepts without concrete form, I believe that the lessons I have learned, throughout a life packed with unusual incident, may well serve him, or her, as well as or better than they have helped me.

Incidentally, because of the definitive warnings given to me by my father I have never used dangerous stimulants or drugs of any kind in order to assist the creative process, and, as soon as it became obvious to me that smoking was a far greater hindrance than help, I gave that up as well.

I am not trying to project a 'goody-goody' image but I simply have never needed such dangerous aids to enhance my imagination. That is the measure of how effective my father's training methods proved to be.

Like most people engaged in creative effort, I have used coffee, tea, and chocolate to refresh my flagging

14

efforts, but I found that the caffeine content of the first two of these stimulants soon wears off, and the sugar content of the third, in excess, is not good for you. I also believe that the effect of them all is largely psychological.

Naturally, I believe that good health is important. The old Latin motto: *Mens Sana in Corpore Sano* (a healthy mind in a healthy body) which adorned the wall of my prep-school gymnasium, is sound advice.

The increased awareness that was the result of all the training given to me by my father provided me with the means of gaining a decent standard of living for my family, as well as offering me the opportunity of choosing an interesting career for myself.

If you look up the word 'career' in most dictionaries, among other definitions it is also described as: 'A rapid progress, downhill.' Often this has seemed to me to be a fair description. My professional career has been rather like a roller-coaster ride, but any success that I have enjoyed has been due to the early opening of my mind and the subsequent opportunities that this provided for me.

Whether I have made the best use of these advantages is, of course, a matter of opinion. However, I am convinced that had I not been given the techniques to open and close my mind safely at will, I would never have emerged, largely unscathed and a mite wiser, from some of the grimmer situations in which I have found myself embroiled.

As you get older, survival gets tougher, but the use of intuition and the rational employment of imagination can help elderly open minded people, just as much as they did in their younger years. That is another excellent reason for keeping yourself alert and vigilant in this rapidly changing world.

My father summed this up for me with some down-to-earth advice: 'Keep your mind and your bowels open and you won't go far wrong!'

What he meant, of course, was to eliminate as much poison, both mental and physical, from my system, as soon as possible. He believed that this was what the Romans meant by their famous maxim. From long experience I am sure that he was right.

Whether the ultra-powerful force of the imagination is used for creativity, as it should be, or to bring about destruction and chaos, is a matter of choice. That is where *motive* becomes the single most important factor in the equation.

Sadly, throughout history, the vitally-important area of decision-making is frequently left to politicians and rabble-rousers like Adolf Hitler, rather than to gifted, but less pragmatic, thinkers and philosophers. As we know, the results have been catastrophic.

As I have grown older, a nagging thought has bothered me. During my sixty-six years of life I have heard people, in moments of crisis, cry out: 'It's all right! Here comes the doctor . . ., or the surgeon, the midwife, the police, the fire brigade, the rescue squad, the paramedics, the skipper, the navigator, the flight engineer, the priest, the rabbi, the imam, or even the plumber.'

But, in all those years, during dire emergencies in peace and war, I have never once heard the words: 'Thank God! the politician has arrived!'

Nor, strangely, have I met anyone else who has ever heard those words. It can't be coincidence, because I have raised this point with so many people, and have always received the same answer.

I am not just being flippant, but in these days, when the importance of many politicians is being overemphasized, through the media of television, radio, and the Press, it gives me the uncomfortable feeling that we are constantly being manipulated and conditioned.

Power, of course, is the name of the game. Power to manipulate the minds of the people, and, in those countries where the State has complete control of the media and freedom of the Press does not exist, disinformation is widely promulgated. However, I believe that we, the people, can learn to protect ourselves and our families from such exploitation.

I think of this as: psychic self-defence. It is my personal early-warning system.

I am convinced that by learning to open up our minds to our inborn nous, and our inherited power of intuition, with its millennia of survival techniques built into our individual genetic systems, we can detect these pressures and block them from being effective.

Moreover, we can pass on the knowledge of these survival techniques to our children, opening their young minds at a far earlier stage, just as my father did for me, instead of stifling their emergent imagination as we tend to do, at our peril, under our present system of education.

At the same time, we can use the sensitivity of our intuition to give us the edge in our daily lives and dramatically improve our own life-style and those of others less fortunate than ourselves.

Therefore, I urge you to open your minds, as I have learnt to open mine, and to start enjoying a far more rewarding life.

To paraphrase Karl Marx: 'Imaginative workers of the world unite. You have nothing to lose but your mental chains!'

CHAPTER ONE

'Cogito, ergo sum'

The phrase 'I think, therefore I am' simplifies the definition of consciousness. It follows that the deeper you think, the more you become aware of the complexity of your mind. You also become conscious of the great effect that other minds have upon your own sense of being.

Children are intensely aware of their surroundings and the aura of love, which should insulate them from the rigours of life, until they can fend for themselves. All too often, even in the supposedly advanced civilization of the Western world, children do not receive the love, care and attention that we would like to see them enjoy.

During the course of my life, it has been an object lesson for me to see children in small tribal societies, in the Amazon jungle, and the Australian outback, receiving more attention, love, and practical teaching in the art of survival, than I have observed in many parts of Europe and the United States. It seemed that the more natural the society or tribal entity, the more the children were appreciated for what they were: the *future*.

Conversely, the more sophisticated the society and the more grossly materialistic the civilized environment became, the less care and love children often seemed to receive.

But, in spite of their lack of these vital basic needs, many uncared for or badly abused children survive, some of them to grow up into an embittered youth. I have known several of these traumatized survivors and I realize how much I owe to the love and care of my parents.

They loved us without suffocating us with cloying senti-mentality, especially Mother, who, oddly enough though she was British, could show emotion more easily than our Peruvian-born father.

Pop was a first-class scientist and a pioneer of aeronau-tical engineering, who after the First World War had been forced to abandon a successful career in seaplane design, due to his recurrent attacks of crippling asthma.

My mother was blessed with a great sense of humour, which my father lacked, but which he later acquired through a process of osmosis, absorbing his British fami-ly's acute sense of the ridiculous.

This ability to laugh at our own misfortunes, rather than at those of others (the classic banana-skin syndrome), has faithfully served my brother and me throughout our lives. Without it, our childhood, in the bourgeois seaside resort of Folkestone, which was supposed to be beneficial for asthmatics, would have been far more difficult than it was.

As two 'Dago' boys, which is how we were labelled, we were treated harshly at our small prep school, which was presided over by a gaunt and severe headmaster with a marked leaning towards sadistic treatment of those chil-dren who didn't measure up to his peculiar standards of British boyhood.

My brother, being six years older, bore the brunt of this mental ill-treatment, stoically and silently, for 'Bro' was far more reserved than I was. In this he took after Pop, whose own boyhood from his arrival in England at the age of thirteen had been spent in the environment of an even more xenophobic Britain, the result of the bigoted Victorian era.

On the other hand, I complained loudly about my treatment at this school, but because I stammered so badly I found it hard to convey to my parents just how much I detested and feared my terrifying headmaster.

It was hard for anyone who did not know this complex and highly intelligent man to understand how quickly he could change his apparently genial personality, which he showed to the parents, to become the sadistic monster that terrified any pupil who was unlucky enough to incur his displeasure.

Why then was it that the parents of the boys didn't spot this unbalanced side of his nature?

The answer is simple. Like many bullies, he had the ability to bamboozle those who had never seen the evil side of his Jekyll-and-Hyde personality. Years later, when comparing notes with my few remaining schoolmates who survived the Second World War, I found that their parents also had acted as apparently illogically as mine had done in continuing to send their children to that school.

My brother and I have come to the conclusion that this strange man was a consummate actor, an ability which he often demonstrated at school plays or when reading books aloud to us during English classes, and that he was obviously able to convince parents of his bona-fide ability to educate their children.

It was only after he went too far with his sadistic treatment of one tough lad, who managed to convince his father of these insufferable quirks in our headmaster's behaviour, that he got into real trouble, but by that time both my brother and I had gone to Eton College.

Nowadays, in Britain, such sadism would be quickly detected and promptly rooted out. It is only now, in our modern society, that the xenophobia of the early part of the twentieth century is being attacked by anti-discrimination organizations. Also, there is a far greater awareness of child-abuse and other sadistic malpractices by some teachers, who, fortunately, are in the minority.

My parents, who could ill afford an expensive public-school education for their sons, sent both of us to Eton for a specific reason; my father's greatest friend since boyhood was a housemaster there.

Years before when they were both fourteen-year-old schoolboys, Pop had made a pact that, one day, he would send his sons to the school where his closest friend would become a teacher, which was the career he had chosen.

William Hope-Jones eventually became a housemaster at Eton. My brother and I have no doubt that, had be become a schoolmaster at a British grammar school or at a Peruvian state school, Pop would have sent us there instead. The odd thing was that at the time of their boyhood pact my father had been absolutely certain that he would have sons, and Uncle Billy had been equally sure that he would be their teacher! Was then their boyhood pact based on prescience?

Eton's heavy fees were met partly by my mother's bridge winnings, a game which she played with professional skill, and partly by her shrewdness in building houses in which we lived happily for a time, until someone would come along and make Mother an offer that she couldn't refuse. Then she would build another house and we would move into that until the cycle was repeated. In all we lived in seven houses in Folkestone.

Our new housemaster was a delightful eccentric, the antithesis of our former, sadistic headmaster. Bill Hope-Jones, as he was thought of, affectionately, by the boys, was the kindest man I have ever known. Selfless and caring, with a giant intellect and a dedicated love of the arts and sciences, this splendid man, who was also my godfather, was rugged and physically fit, like my Folkestone schoolmaster, but there blessedly the resemblance ended.

Both my brother and I are very grateful to Uncle Billy, as we knew him, for repairing most of the damage that our former tormentor had wrought. Furthermore, it was my godfather who saw to it that my dreadful stammer was treated successfully at Eton by a visiting speech-therapist, who had been one of his former pupils.

I am also grateful to that excellent speech-trainer, Harry Burgess, for ridding me of a form of mental torture, that only those who stammer badly will appreciate. (I have dealt at length with this subject in my book: *A Shy Person's Guide to Life*.)

There is no doubt that my severe impediment, which amounted to a near-total speech-block, had been aggravated, if not induced, by that Folkestone headmaster, and it was cured largely because of the kindness of my Etonian housemaster.

I only mention this early part of my life because it had a direct bearing on the development of my imagination and the consequent ability that I gained to cope with the mental handicaps, caused by my unhappy prep-school experiences. These consisted of my appalling stammer and an acute fear of authority which Uncle Billy rectified in a surprisingly short time, thereby making my boyhood a much happier experience.

But the course of events that completely altered my life was my father's decision to investigate, scientifically, what were then generally known as psychic phenomena or the study of the supernormal.

Pop's radical decision had been brought about by some extraordinary and puzzling evidence that he had received in 1931, during a seance held in a bungalow near Hawkinge, a village perched high up on the North Downs above Folkestone. I have dealt fully with this in my book, *The Door Marked Summer*, but for the sake of new readers, I will briefly refer to it.

Apparently during this sitting, at which about fifteen people were present, my father had been given precise evidence of a romantic relationship he had had in his teens, with a young actress – a situation which nobody there could have known about, as my father was a complete stranger to them all.

The evidence involved the definitive description of a failed theatrical venture, and an enforced public auction of all the unfortunate actors' and actresses' possessions, which had been held on the stage of a provincial theatre, at Bolton in Lancashire.

This had occurred in 1905 and the message was: to thank my father for his kindness and generosity on that sad occasion. As Pop explained it later to us: he and another

23

teenage South-American friend, who had accompanied him on the disastrous tour of the provinces, had arranged for the theatre's stage-manager to buy back at the auction all this young actress's personal possessions, and to leave them in her dressing-room with a note and enough money to cover her train fare back to London.

Both Pop and his friend had been too shy to face their actress friend, as they knew she would have refused their help, so they had decided that this was the best method of showing her their affection, in a practical way.

They had then taken the train for London, before she could thank them for their kind gesture, and, as Fate would have it, they had never seen their young friend again.

This bizarre message so impressed my father, because nobody present could have known of this incident from his past, that he decided to devote his enforced retirement which he found irksome, to the scientific investigation of what is now known as the paranormal.

So, in his early thirties, my father became one of that small band of pioneer parapsychologists, like Sir Arthur Conan Doyle, Air-Marshal Sir Hugh Dowding, and Hannen Swaffer, the critic and journalist, who, in those days, were regarded as dangerous eccentrics, dabbling in the occult, and probably in league with the devil, as well.

Because Pop never did anything by halves, my brother and I became his guinea pigs.

This may sound callous, but anyone who knew my father's thorough and unbiased methods of research would realize that we were in the safest possible hands. Pop would never have put his family at risk. He just wanted us to share in any positive results, right from the start; so this is where the story of the opening of my mind really begins.

I have dealt, in considerable detail, with my father's researches and our family's involvement with paranormal phenomena, in my two previous books, so I will confine myself to describing, briefly, the sort of manifestations that I personally witnessed, or had described to me, first-hand, by my father and his trusted colleagues.

These formed the solid basis for the development of my own, extrasensory, awareness.

Most of the phenomena, which I experienced between 1931 and 1939, were manifested in our own home, where my father could impose strict control over the conditions, and where trickery and faking on the part of visiting mediums were least likely to occur. Therefore, the bulk of these strange manifestations were genuine and for me in particular, it proved to be a time of wonders.

I was present on many occasions, when my father, mother, brother and occasionally a guest medium sat round a heavy Victorian pedestal table, which often levitated, in *full* light, and then proceeded to spell out a code, rocking through the letters of the alphabet rapidly enough to make this a viable, if somewhat bizarre, method of communication.

It sounds a lot of mumbo-jumbo but, strangely enough, these seances were free of any phoney air of mystery and that solid pedestal table at times seemed to assume a definite personality of its own. This was in much the same way that a skilled puppeteer can so manipulate his wooden marionettes, that they appear to have characters of their own. Having worked with many talented puppeteers, I have seen this done, many times.

That weighty piece of furniture seemed to become 'alive' under our fingers, once they touched its highly-polished wooden surface, and the messages that the table spelled out were so evidential and, in many cases, so *accurately* predictive about future events, that I came to accept this strange phenomenon as being completely genuine.

After all, why should it have been anything else? Most of the time only my family was involved, so why should we try to fool each other? It certainly would have been impossible to fake the levitation in *full light*, and none of us could have deliberately manipulated that heavy table, when only our fingertips rested lightly upon it.

Furthermore, the sittings often were conducted during the summer months, in sunlight, with the lace curtains drawn. It was only in the winter, that we held sittings in reduced light, and even then the room was well lit by the drawing-room fire, which certainly was bright enough so that we could see everything that was going on. I remember that clearly, because I was nervous of the dark and the firelight was most comforting.

The strangest thing about these family sittings was that, as each Communicator finished and another personality apparently took over the manipulation of the table, we could sense a complete change in the way that the rapidly rocking table spelled out the messages. That is not so hard to believe if you have been trained in transmitting and receiving Morse code, when you learned that every operator of a Morse-key has a completely different technique or signature, as we called it during the war.

In fact, this difference in speed and style of operating a Morse-key actually identified each individual operator of an 'S' phone, the portable clandestine transmitter, used by the wartime Resistance in Europe. If the wrong Morse-key signature was received by the control operator, in London, the chances were that the message was a fake. Quite often, an Abwehr (German counter-espionage) wireless-operator, masquerading as a Resistance radio-man, would be detected quickly by the highly-skilled operators at British Signals Headquarters.

Over a period of ten years, that heavy table rocked out some remarkable messages, in which the predictive element of prophecy was *100* per cent accurate! This may seem an extravagant claim to make, but I assure you that it is true, and my later wartime involvement with British Intelligence and the nature of clandestine radio-transmissions, confirmed what I had experienced as a boy when I sat with my family round that strangely animated Victorian table.

Looking at it, objectively, it was a crude method of communication, but I have seen other devices, which were far more sophisticated, yet proved to be nowhere near as effective. The levitation effect also was quite startling, with the heavy table flying about, with no possibility whatsoever of faking *that* phenomenon. It certainly was an exciting introduction to the world of the paranormal!

Besides our home circle, from which the best evidence seemed to come, I was taken to a large number of different demonstrations of supernormal phenomena. Sadly, a lot of these were about as convincing as amateur conjuring, and some were excruciatingly bad. But I also witnessed a few outstanding demonstrations of genuine clairvoyance and clairaudience, some remarkable psychometry and even instances of physical phenomena, such as an impressive transfiguration, where the medium's face completely changed its appearance in the presence of some twenty witnesses, in full summer afternoon sunlight.

This demonstration by a Mrs Enid Balmer, which I witnessed in our own home, on that sunny day, in 1938, was completely convincing and totally *inexplicable*, by the tenets of physical science.

Like my family, I was sure this was *not* a case of mass hypnotism, because the guests at this particular sitting were mainly sceptical friends, who would have been difficult to hypnotize, *en masse*, even if the medium had been an exceptional mesmerist. Moreover, apart from a short prayer at the start of the demonstration, Mrs Balmer did not speak a word until the end of the hour long sitting. Therefore, we can discount mass-hypnotism.

The transfiguration was remarkable, because so many different faces manifested, appearing quite clearly in a kind of ectoplasmic mist, which seemed to surround the medium's face. Furthermore, these manifesting entities, which ranged from a bewigged judge, through a number of contrasting adult male and female faces of different ages including a young girl, with flaming red hair, were all clearly recognized by one or other of the twenty or so sitters.

Photographs which were taken during the course of the sitting appeared to be badly fogged, as though by X-rays. Three skilled photographers, including my father, were involved and twelve pictures were taken by each operator – a total of thirty-six exposures in all.

Yet, only the *first* and *last* pictures, taken at the very beginning and at the end of the sitting, were free from this strange fogging effect, indicating the presence of some form of intense radiation.

That afternoon demonstration was mind-bending.

During those ten years of long sessions of investigation into this strange world of the paranormal, I began to develop the sensitivity of my mind to a degree that I would never have thought possible when I was that frightened little boy at prep school.

Certain mediums and psychics, who became my teachers and mentors, stand out in my memory as being especially impressive.

For example, Eddie Partridge, a kindly middle-aged grocer, kept a tiny corner shop in Dover, and thereby helped his neighbours through the Depression by offering them endless credit. As he told my father, he was able to do so only because: 'The Lord Provided'. I believe him for, somehow, he never went bankrupt and he was always able to provide enough for everybody among his customers during the awful years of the Depression, without dunning any of his impoverished clients, who paid him whenever they could.

Eddie was one of the most remarkable mediums and healers I ever met.

In addition, he showed me how to use the natural in-born ability of my mind to release my *overmind*, as I came to think of it, from my immediate material surroundings and to soar wherever I wished to go, without the danger of losing control and being unable to return to my body.

This is a very real peril, which I firmly believe could account for a number of unexplained deaths, when the victims were known to have been engaged in paranormal experiments along these lines. However, the more prosaic coroner's verdict of the cause of death in these cases, was often given as 'Apoplexy'.

These mental journeys may sound bizarre, but nowadays 'OOBEs' (out-of-the-body-experiences) are far more widely accepted than they were during the thirties.

Pop had a very close relationship with Eddie Partridge and conducted a large number of closely-monitored experiments with this extraordinary man, at some of which I was present. I can vouch for the fact that Eddie's cheerful down-to-earth personality, if you can use such an expression in his case, made these demonstrations of paranormal phenomena seem as natural as breathing. I have no doubt whatsoever that he was completely genuine.

Another plus on our side as investigators of this strange world of the powers of the human mind was that Pop since boyhood had been a keen amateur conjuror, practised in the arts of sleight-of-hand and stage-illusions, so he was well equipped to spot any tricks being employed. We also had two family friends, who were both adept members of the Inner Magic Circle of British professional and amateur stage magicians. These experienced colleagues were present at a number of our sittings, with various outstanding mediums under test, and pronounced themselves satisfied that they had no logical explanation for the extraordinary phenomena being produced.

At one sitting, in Dover, during a seance in Eddie's small sitting-room behind the shop, my mother, who was by nature a sceptic, was levitated and carried across a large kitchen table round which the sitting was being conducted. She was safely deposited on the lap of a sitter, on the other side of the small room.

Mother was a large woman of Junoesque proportions, and when it happened she was so startled that she gasped out loud. I was not present at the time of this extraordinary event, but Ma told me afterwards that she was convinced that the phenomenon was genuine.

Furthermore, only Eddie and his equally small wife, 'Biny', plus Pop and one other sitter, Eddie's stocky brother-in-law, a local fisherman, were present at this sitting, which took place in near total darkness. But even in full light it would have been extremely difficult for these lightly-built people to have lifted Mother's not inconsiderable weight and carried her right across the wide table, to deposit her gently on the lap of the sitter on the opposite side; all of which took place, in just a few seconds.

As Ma, like Pop, was a completely truthful person to whom deliberate lying was total anathema I accepted her account of what happened, unreservedly.

Another extraordinary experience, which I shared with my father and Eddie during the silence of a late summer night in 1939, took place in the middle of a small Kentish wood, when this wonderful man, with one gentle, almost inaudible sound, somewhere between a soft whistle and a whispered word, woke up every animal, bird, reptile and insect, asleep in the warm darkness. That spontaneous and joyous chorus of Nature welcoming a much-loved friend was the single most amazing thing I have ever heard, and that magical experience has remained with me throughout my life as a treasured memory. It was almost as though Pan, himself, had entered the wood.

Eddie Partridge was a very remarkable man. I never met his like again!

Arthur Bhaduri, a frail and gentle Indian friend, was another remarkable medium, whom Pop investigated and found to be completely genuine. Arthur, who was clairvoyant, taught me how to use a black, earthenware bowl, filled with water, as a focus to concentrate my mind and to release my Overmind to wander at will.

He told me that this technique, which he had learnt in the Orient, had been used by the Ancient Egyptians for scrying, the art of viewing far beyond the normal range of vision, irrespective of time and space. The way I now remember my experience with Arthur's scrying bowl, was that it was like looking at a modern black television screen.

I sat comfortably with the bowl in front of me on a table, the lights in the room were lowered and the shades were drawn. I then focused my gaze into the darkness of the water. Almost immediately, the black bowl seemed to fill my horizon and shortly after I felt my mind release itself, so that the depths of the bowl became its ambience. Pictures, like small crowded scenes, formed inside the darkness and these changed quite rapidly, with many different faces becoming apparent. It was absolutely fascinating and all the time I had no sensation of unease, because my father's Indian friend was a guru and I knew that had I become distressed he immediately would have safely returned me to full consciousness.

However, I would not have cared to have undergone the experience alone, and I would strongly recommend that nobody should try this experiment on their own. Nevertheless, on that occasion when I first practised the art of scrying with Arthur Bhaduri, I felt refreshed by the experience and had no sense of fear whatsoever.

Arthur explained to me that scrying was one reason why Ancient Egypt had remained inviolate from invasion for many centuries. This highly intelligent Indian scholar told me that the Priesthood had used this method of scrying, to scan the full extent of the borders of Upper and Lower Egypt, supposedly in much the same way that nowadays we use Radar to give early warning of the approach of aircraft, hostile or otherwise.

According to Arthur Bhaduri, a twenty-four-hour vigil was kept by these watchers in the Temples, and, moreover, these scryers also had the ability to communicate, *mentally*, with their opposite numbers inside the Temples of the two capital cities and could pass on warnings, so that the Pharoah could instantly move his military forces, in order to counter any threat. This may sound implausible,

31

but then in the thirties our present system of early-warning Radar would have seemed equally impossible.

At that time I was very interested in Egyptology, and I knew from my studies of the work of Doctor Wallis Budge and other well-known authorities on Ancient Egypt that this great civilization had been deeply aware of the powers of the human mind. I also had complete confidence in Arthur Bhaduri's knowledge and his extraordinary mediumistic abilities. Therefore, it seemed to me that as he had demonstrated to me the effectiveness of this method of remote viewing what he told me was a plausible and valid reason for that long period when Ancient Egypt had enjoyed such a long period of prosperity and freedom from attack.

Be that as it may, Arthur's method of scrying with the black, water-filled bowl, taught me yet another effective method of releasing my Overmind from its material surroundings, and in my imagination viewing the realms of the *Human Collective Unconscious* as Carl Gustav Jung described it or, as I think of it, *The Universal Overmind*.

In my previous books I have outlined my personal definitions of *Brain*, *Mind*, *Overmind* and *Universal Overmind*, so here is a brief recapitulation of these terms.

For me the *Brain* is the receiver, through the faculties of sight, hearing, touch, smell and taste, of all the impressions caused by events and happenings, which directly or indirectly affect the body of which it is a part and which it controls.

The brain also is a transmitter, through its nervous systems, and it rapidly reacts to these constantly changing circumstances, mainly *instinctively*, but also with the rational-thinking process, derived from experience.

This, for me, is the process of survival.

I believe that the *Mind*, which is generated by and sustained by the brain, is also metaphysical, in the sense that it can exist as *another* dimension of the brain. Therefore I visualize it as a co-relative, co-existent, parallel entity to the brain.

32

Furthermore, I believe that the mind is subject to an extent to the brain's hereditary genetic factors, including race-memory, and also that, like its host and lifetime partner, the mind is moulded and conditioned by learning and experience.

Moreover, my own paranormal experiences lead me to the conclusion that the mind is capable of extra-dimensional thought, in the form of *Overmind*, manifesting through the imagination and the unconscious mind. Therefore under certain conditions, which are not always present, it has the capability of extrasensory perception.

During its time of incarnation, the mind is totally dependent on the brain and body for survival.

I believe that after death, the mind leaves the body, to exist extra-dimensionally as a separate entity in the form of *Overmind*.

It then becomes part of the *Universal Overmind*, or, as Carl Gustav Jung described it, the *Collective Human Unconscious*. This is made up of the totality of *all* past and present human experience, and this may well be the original source of energy from which the mind comes.

In other words, this recycling of mind energy seems to me to be like the return of the physical body to the earth of its origin. For me it is the reunion of the mind and its *Overmind*, with the realm, or plane of existence of all *Mind Energy*, or if you prefer it *Spirit*.

I am no guru, with some new and blinding revelation, nor do I pretend that this simplistic statement is in any way a scientific theory, nor is it provable by empiric, repeatable, experiments. But, in my terms, as an imaginative person who has experienced a significant amount of paranormal phenomena, it does seem to make sense.

It is, if you like, my *Belief*.

I think that, throughout our lives, we are dealing with and are ourselves a part of vast fields of energy, which have the characteristics of interacting, and inter-reacting, as cause and effect, both physically and metaphysically, within the parameters of what Einstein has defined as: our continuum of 4-Dimensional Space-Time, in which Time is the *Fourth* dimension.

For me learning to project my mind through the process of scrying was one of the most significant of those paranormal experiences.

However, as I have mentioned before, there are attendant dangers to scrying, and I believe that these experiments should never be conducted alone, but only in the presence of a trustworthy and qualified friend, who can monitor the whole operation and help the experimenter to return safely to the body, should any signs of distress or anxiety become apparent. I shall discuss the techniques involved later on in this book.

I feel very strongly that to mix this type of paranormal activity with the use of drugs, *of any kind*, is tantamount to committing mental or even *actual* physical suicide.

I have no doubts whatsoever about giving this warning!

Since those early days I have experimented with and learnt the basic rules governing other forms of scrying. These have included Tarot, the earliest form of playing cards, which are believed to have been based on the Ancient Egyptian archetypal forms of the collective unconscious mind, i.e. the universal overmind.

Apparently Sir Alec Guinness, one of our greatest actors, also experimented with Tarot, finding it so dangerously obsessive that he wisely stopped reading them. He describes this fully in his delightful autobiography.

I can well understand his objection to using this method of divination, since I have found that *all* methods of scrying or divining, unless rigidly controlled under ideal conditions, have this built-in danger.

Whether the scryer is using Tarot, the 'I Ching' (the ingenious Chinese *Book of Changes* developed long before the Christian era by the Emperor Wu Li), the Runes of the Norsemen, or simpler forms of divination, such as the Ouija board, with all its attendant perils, or the upturned glass, or even the basic 'Yes-No' system of the dowser's pendulum, the danger is always the same.

34

Over-dependence on *any* form of communication with the unconscious mind and its *Archetypes* of the collective unconscious, those shadowy but none the less real creations of centuries of human belief in their existence is bound to weaken the Will and lead to all sorts of psychological troubles, ranging from a nervous breakdown to total insanity. Possession and obsession are close companions, once the Human Will is suborned and disorientated.

I have known unfortunate people, who became too closely involved with these methods of prophecy and then found it impossible to stop using them.

These foci of the mind are by their very nature symbolic and once their use is understood they are best left alone, especially by those who are nervous or weak-willed. Sadly, the very nature of this symbolism in divining is its most attractive feature and particularly appeals to those who are indecisive and habitually unsure of themselves. They feel that these methods give them some sort of advantage, in avoiding having to make decisions for themselves, and therein lies the greatest danger in the misuse, or over-use, of these methods.

Obviously, the same caveats apply to any techniques which are used to focus the unconscious mind and to open the doors to the limitless worlds of the imagination, in learning to safely navigate inner space, and I must stress that lack of care and attention to the security of these voyages can bring disaster, as surely as the tragedy that cost the lives of seven splendid astronauts, aboard the ill-fated space-shuttle *Challenger*.

All this may seem overly melodramatic and solely written for effect. I assure you that this is not so!

I have been a keen sailor for many years and would no more think of commencing a sea voyage, or even estuary cruising, without first taking adequate safety precautions, from having the correct charts of the cruising area aboard, and thoroughly understanding how to use them for constantly updating my estimated position by taking compass-bearings, sextant and radio bearings, to having sufficient life-jackets and a properly equipped life-raft aboard, complete with distress flares, emergency food pack and a proper supply of fresh water.

Over-reaction? From some frightening personal experiences I don't think so and neither does the RNLI (Royal National Lifeboat Institution) of which I am a life member. These weatherwise seamen have often told me that if more amateur yachtsmen were trained in seamanship and were properly equipped with the necessary life-saving apparatus, they would not have to witness so many unnecessary tragedies around Britain's coasts.

In all my years of messing about in boats in all weathers, I have seen enough of this sort of needless disaster, to know that our experienced lifeboatmen are right.

I have learnt the hard way that there is only one safe way to fly an aeroplane, or to sail a small ship, and that is *professionally*. The same rules apply to mental voyaging in the infinite worlds of the Imagination.

CHAPTER TWO

Inspiration, intuition and the muse

I would never have survived the war, but for the previous exhaustive training, by my father and others, which had succeeded in opening my mind, and had taught me to trust my intuition.

Time and again that split-second of foreknowledge literally saved my life and my reason.

When the Second World War finally ground to a halt, I found myself to be an out-of-work civilian, and a badly shaken one at that, with grim memories of my time in the RAF still haunting me. Having seen more than enough killing and destruction by the misuse of science, I was determined not to pursue a scientific career, as my father had wanted me to do.

My elder brother, who was an artist, had been in the Army, as an anti-aircraft gunner, for six years, whereas it had taken me almost eighteen months from the start of the war to join the Royal Air Force. This was due to a ridiculous xenophobic prejudice against people like my brother and myself because our father was Peruvian, although both of us had been born in Britain with dual-nationality.

During the war, Pop and Mother, who was British, were forced to leave the south coast without recompense and to sell our home in Folkestone for a fraction of what it was worth. All this was because father was officially an Alien – from a friendly neutral country at that. The fact that both their sons were volunteers and served in the Forces didn't count in their favour and

I still feel a lingering sense of outrage at their treatment.

In 1946, when I was demobilized and for no other reason than it seemed to be a good idea at the time, I decided to try my luck in show business, as a comedian. I was twenty-four years old and only knew a few dirty jokes, which every other serviceman knew as well. Totally unequipped for a career in comedy, except for my vivid pictorial imagination, which my father had helped me develop, I let my mind reach out for something different in humour, preferably a routine that no other comedian had used.

Using the special techniques for opening my mind that I had been taught I set about this daunting task.

As a yardstick, to test the effectiveness of my recall of the great days of movie comedy of the twenties and early thirties, I started to scan the whole spectrum of my memory of the slapstick screen humour which I had enjoyed so much since my early childhood.

For a week, I mentally reviewed those masterpieces of visual comedy. It was an extraordinary experience, which proved to me how effectively the cinema had implanted these images in my young mind.

As Lenin said: 'Of all the arts of Propaganda, the most important one to us is the cinema!'

Whatever one thinks of his politics, there's no denying that he was extremely clever, for that perceptive remark was made in 1921, when the cinema was black and white and silent. It was a remarkable prophecy!

My mental marathon of joyous recall of screen comedy didn't prove to be as difficult a task as one might imagine in these days of videotape recordings, because, since the age of four, my young mind had been brought up on the movies.

All that information was firmly implanted in my Unconscious Mind.

Moreover, my father's training in developing my visual imagination had been so effective that I was able to complete that detailed comedy review in just seven days. I didn't realize it at the time, but it was quite a feat of memory, being almost total recall!

When I had finished this mental retrospective of the work of the giants of comedy, I had a firm base from which to start developing my own style of humour, for I had no intention of consciously plagiarizing their original ideas.

Of course, there was no way I could reproduce on stage the sort of hilariously imaginative tricks and effects that these creative comedians had performed on film. Moreover, most of them were highly-skilled acrobats, like Buster Keaton, Charlie Chaplin, Harold Lloyd, and Laurel and Hardy, and I wasn't particularly athletic. So I had no way of duplicating their wonderful physical comedy. In addition, there were plenty of established music-hall comedians already doing impressions of Charlie Chaplin, ranging from excellent to unbelievably bad.

Whatever I decided to perform had to be different from the work of my screen heroes, while at the same time I could use them as perfect examples of how visual comedy should be performed. By the end of that week of happy recall, I was ready to start 'Freescanning', as I came to call the act of letting my imagination run wild.

Immediately, a whole parade of funny ideas started to pass across the inner screen of my mind. Unfortunately, most of these original comedy images and concepts were totally impractical. I would have needed to be a wealthy man to have a fraction of the many bizarre props that I visualized in my imagination. That was out of the question! So I started to scale down my ideas to something that I could afford to buy and the prop that I finally decided to use for an original mime act was a simple, crook-handled walking-stick.

Using the vivid pictures I had conjured up in my mind, I worked out an act, in which an imaginative young man, while waiting for his girlfriend, visualizes his walking-stick as various objects, such as a sword, with which he defends himself, like Errol Flynn, against numerous attackers.

The next moment, he sees himself as a big-game fisherman hooking a giant fighting-fish. This hurls him all over the stage, as he tries to reel it in. In a wildly energetic sequence of comedy-mimes, the stick became the key to each different situation, taking over the young man, like Frankenstein's monster.

To my amazement it worked. But the act required far more setting up than I had supposed. Music-hall audiences weren't nearly as imaginative as I had hoped, and, although a lot of youngsters among them laughed and applauded, the older, more conservative people in the audience sat in stunned silence.

Evidently my act was too radically different for them to accept. They had never seen anything like it, and, apparently, this was a great disadvantage. That was the first lesson I learned.

However, the stage staff at the theatres where I tried out my act encouraged me to keep on with it.

My short, eight-minute, performance also needed suitable background music and that meant more expense, to get band-parts specially written for the music-hall orchestras. So, after performing at a couple of smaller provincial theatres, I looked around for a similar idea, equally original, but on much simpler lines, needing neither an introduction, nor music.

By sheer accident, I found the perfect prop, which turned out to be the broken back of an antique chair.

It all happened when I accidentally broke one of my brother's precious chairs. Not that the wooden chair itself was particularly valuable, but it happened to be one of only three chairs that my brother and sister-in-law possessed. Like me, they were flat broke. However, they were very nice about my clumsiness.

An important contributory factor to this fortuitous accident was that both of them were skilled artists, with excellent visual imaginations.

Laughing our heads off, the three of us spontaneously mimed many different uses for that broken chair-back, until I suddenly realized that here was the perfect prop for the comedy act I had been seeking.

Had the chair-back not broken in that particular way, at that particular time, giving our three imaginative minds the opportunity to see the many different objects that it could represent, and had I not already explored the possibilities of miming with my walking-stick, I would not have found myself in possession of this new and completely original act, which started me on my long career in show business.

I find it hard to believe that it was all just coincidence.

It actually took me over three months of rehearsal to put it all together, so that it became a smooth, apparently effortless flow of original comedy-mime. From start to finish, the whole routine lasted exactly *four minutes*, during which time I linked the wildly energetic mime, by giving a melodramatic, nonsensical political speech, while I was being thrown around, apparently uncontrollably, by the different objects and bizarre situations generated by the broken chair-back.

In those four, action-packed minutes it became a runaway road-drill, a pillory, an axe with which I chopped down a tree, the rudder of a ship in a storm, a giant comb, a mirror, handcuffs, the bars of a prison cell, a plough, and numerous other ridiculous objects that projected me into a whole series of slapstick situations, throwing me around the stage like a rubber ball.

Surprisingly, apart from a few bruises, suffered during these violent antics, I survived quite well, for by this time I had learnt to do 'prat-falls', i.e. comedy tumbling without killing myself. But it was hard work, twice nightly! Though the whole sequence of the act only took those few energetic minutes, by the end of it I was completely exhausted, having put my all into every performance.

Happily, it was an enormous success, from the moment I first performed it in public, at the Servicemen's Nuffield

Centre club, where I tried out my acts, to my 1947 opening in the West End of London, in a show called *Starlight Roof* at the London Hippodrome, where to my amazement I stole many of the Press notices.

That four-minute act never failed me once. In fact, it continued with equal success during the following ten years, when it formed the opening part of my music-hall performances, which took me right round the world: a total of well over five thousand demanding performances.

Frankly, I could not perform it today, to save my life. I just don't have the energy any more, nor the breath.

I mention it because it is a practical example of what part imagination, plus a bit of luck, played in completely transforming my life. That ridiculous broken back of an old chair turned me into a successful professional comedian, starting me off on a forty-two-year career in show business, taking me round the world, many times.

Therefore, I claim that had I not been encouraged to open my mind and to control my thoughts by channelling them into a creative state, there is no way that I could have made such a rapid transition into becoming an original and successful comedian in the West End of London, then the show-business capital of the world.

It is even more surprising, when you consider that I was completely untrained in comedy, or in any other form of show-business expertise, apart from a short spell in the legitimate theatre, playing Shakespeare, just before joining the RAF.

I am not boasting, but merely pointing out the extraordinary ways of Destiny.

From all those years of training with my father, and other mentors, I had learnt that our inner senses are far more acute than our outer ones. But, sadly, we have allowed them to become blunted and dulled by our ultra-materialistic way of life.

However, in the course of my world-wide travels, over the last forty years, I have found that this is not the case, where the natural peoples of the world are concerned. I have worked with a number of what Western anthropologists would describe as primitive tribal groups, and found them to be far from primitive, mentally, though their material lives lacked most of the material benefits of modern Western civilization. These extraordinary people live close to nature, much like their earliest ancestors, and, consequently, their survival senses are far more acute than the ones we use, in our supposedly civilized world.

The ones I met were located in Africa, the Middle East, South America, Australia and New Zealand. These remarkable survivors from the Golden Age of early man had retained most of their ancestors' acute extrasensory ability. From the first moment I had contact with them, they recognized the rapport between us, sensing that my mind, like theirs, was open. From then on, our communication was total, friendly and completely unaffected by the apparent difference in our lifestyles.

My friend, the late Danny Kaye, once told me that he had experienced exactly similar reactions, during his many world-wide missions for the United Nations children's fund. Apparently, being a clown has certain advantages.

Whether these splendid people were mountain Indians of the High Sierra, or the jungle tribes of the Amazonas, nomadic Aborigines in Australia, the delightful Maori people of New Zealand, tribesmen in Africa, or the Bedouin of the Middle East, when I met them something passed between us, like a current of electricity. For each of us understood the awareness and goodwill of the other.

It was always a wonderful experience and, many years later, that wise man, Sir Laurens Van Der Post, also told me that he had sensed the same instant rapport with the Bushmen of the Kalahari.

I cannot pretend to possess the wisdom and spiritual awareness of Sir Laurens, nor to be as adept a clown as Danny Kaye, but it was exciting to hear them both confirm my feelings about contacts with the natural peoples of the earth.

I have been very lucky indeed to have used my earnings, from writing and performing in show business, once my family had been well looked after and given number one priority, to travel extensively.

Sometimes, I was accompanied on long business trips by my wife, and, during a two-year engagement in Australia, by two of our eldest children and our beloved friend, 'Nursie', as well. During those trips, we met many of these wonderful natural people, whose minds, from birth, had been fully opened to the magic of their inner senses.

Would that part of their inherited natural wisdom and sensitivity would rub-off on some of the politicians who, at present, are in charge of our Fate.

Often during the course of my life, both in peace and war, I have demonstrably been shown the power of the human mind, to create original concepts and, apparently, to receive inspiration from some, not yet understood, external source. Many times, I have received warnings of coming events, or have been impressed to take a certain course of action, which has resulted in a dramatic change in my life; a sort of mental crossroads.

Usually, these flashes of intuition, or inspiration, are completely involuntary, as though I am being guided by some higher intelligence, and there are many different theories to account for this, some of which I will discuss later in the book. For the time being, let it suffice to say that I do believe in *Guidance* of some sort and rely on it heavily, when I am in danger or in a crisis.

This guidance has never let me down, but it only manifests *after* I have done everything possible to find the answer to my problems. Then, and only then, that familiar still small voice inside my mind tells me what to do, or, in a clear flash of imagery, I see the answer to my problem projected on to the inner screen of my mind.

Another practical example of this intuitive clairvoyance (which only means clear-seeing) came to me in Cardiff, South Wales, in a theatre dressing-room. It was late 1954 when, while daydreaming, I saw the entire three-dimensional image of an 'Invisible Flea Circus', seemingly projected on to the grey wall of the dressing room. This objective form of clairvoyance, or if you prefer it, intense visual imagination, in this case was complete with all the miniature working apparatus that moved to indicate the presence of an unseen insect, as the 'Invisible Flea' apparently jumped around in the sand. It also seemed to push a ball up a slope, climb a ladder to a diving-platform and, from the board, dive into a cup of water, sending a splash high into the air.

This ridiculous vision later became one of my most popular acts. I designed many different versions of these miniature 'invisible' scenarios, which I used in over fifty of my television shows. In fact, a number of performers have copied this distinctive, original act, and it has been played by others on BBC television programmes, even when the producers in the Corporation well knew that the original idea, the whole concept, the design and copyright was mine.

It was not one of my happiest memories of the British Broadcasting Corporation.

This example demonstrates the practical value of original thinking. It also pinpoints how risky it is to talk about your ideas, until they are as fully protected as possible.

At this point the question arises: How original is original?

Conventional semantics, well-known pictorial elements, familiar musical sounds, and generally accepted symbols or notation, such as those used in mathematics, or musical notation, naturally form part of each individual method of creative thinking. These basic elements, which are the tools used by original thinkers, must be, by their very nature, already in existence in the Collective Human Unconscious.

45

This gives plagiarists an air of validity to their argument: that there is nothing new under the sun, and, therefore, that they have the right to use the work of the creative mind, without acknowledgement or payment for all the originator's effort, stress and hard work that went into it.

That is why the law of copyright came into existence: to protect the original creator of a work, and to treat it as a property.

However, it is not the basic conventions that give originality to creative work, but its individual arrangement, which makes it different and original, thereby bearing the unmistakable stamp of its creator.

An original painting by Leonardo da Vinci is accepted as a true 'Leonardo', because the hand of the great artist is so distinctive, yet a similar work by the School of Leonardo, though highly skilled, does not bear the same outstanding brushwork of the master.

The plays by William Shakespeare, though probably influenced by the advice of contemporaries, like Sir Francis Bacon, are instantly recognizable as original works of genius, from the pen of the great English playwright and poet. Are we then to deny their originality, by arguing that Will Shakespeare was, after all, only using contemporary semantics in writing them down, and that, therefore, we are entitled to use them, without acknowledgement to the genius of their author?

In the case of these dead masters, the copyright has, long since, passed into public domain, but we still acknowledge their original creativity. Today, however, there is far too much plagiarism and outright thievery of the work of original thinkers, writers and other creative minds, being perpetrated by those whose own restricted and amoral thinking is completely lacking in originality.

Sadly, plagiarists often manoeuvre their way into positions of considerable administrative power, where they can act as a filter for the work of other people's creative minds, and browse at leisure among original works, which are, in good faith, being sent to them for assessment. In other words: they are betraying the trust, which their position gives them. To my mind this is plain and simple fraud.

It has been an unhappy experience of mine, many times over, and therefore I stress the importance of protecting the work of original artists and writers, as best we can.

The golden rule is always to keep a dated, provable (i.e. in the hands of a bank manager, or lawyer), *sealed* copy of your work, at the same time as you send the original, and then only by registered post or recorded delivery, for assessment by an accredited representative of the firm for whom you wish to work. It has been my experience that this precaution, sadly, can apply as much to large commercial enterprises, as it does to some small firm of producers, publishers, or individual entrepreneurs.

I have made a deliberate issue of these circumstances to bring home to the reader the *real* value of original creative thinking, not only in show business and the arts, but in the everyday commercial world as well.

I believe that if we are to come through these precarious times and survive as a species, there is a vital need for creative thinking and for the protection of all those valuable original thoughts, when written down and copyrighted, from their misuse, by those who seek to profit by them, or, as in the case of Albert Einstein's work, to pervert them for their own nefarious purposes.

In the final analysis, the truth is always the best way to face any problem.

This is why I believe so firmly in the prime importance of opening the mind as soon and as much as possible, in order to face life with the most knowledge we can acquire.

The more we exercise our imagination and our latent creativity, the more chance we have of survival, of freedom of choice in our careers and life-styles, and less chance of letting ourselves be misled, bamboozled and conned by those who, somehow, usually by our own

47

neglect in not closely examining their credentials, have set themselves up in authority over us.

Which is another reason why I have written this book; to try and pass on to others some of the hard-won lessons that I have learned, during my sixty-six years of life on earth.

CHAPTER THREE

Creativity is magic

For me the best definition of magic is: 'The ability to alter future circumstances by the exercise of will'.

This is what the proper use of creativity is about.

Is magic a ridiculous self-delusion, the result of fantastic mumbo-jumbo? Certainly not the magic that I know!

Consider for a moment what the ancient magicians were doing. Put at its simplest, they were searching for the Gnosis (knowledge), i.e. they were looking for the truth in Nature.

Magicians like Paracelsus were the forerunners of our modern physicists. Yet, in our present nuclear age of microchip technology, the uninitiated, when looking at the complexity of linear and non-linear equations, without knowledge of mathematics and calculus, can only see a maze of meaningless symbols, a jumble of figures and letters, Arabic, Greek, Latin and what have you.

In other words, the lay person is looking at formulae, every bit as weird as the rituals in any arcane Devil's Bible would have seemed to a frightened sorcerer's apprentice.

Yet, to the initiated, these complex sets of letters, symbols and figures are arranged in a way that plainly lays out in front of the mathematician each step of a formalized argument, or theory. For those who understand the symbols, there is nothing mystical about mathematics.

So it was and still is with magic, which is only a theoretical method, or series of mental formulae for focusing the power of the mind. Often, modern technologists are as guilty of human vanity as the magicians of old, and cannot resist mystifying the lay-person with the complexity of their art.

But the facts are undeniable. Magic was the forerunner of physics, alchemy was the progenitor of chemistry, astrology gave birth to astronomy, and mesmerism was the key to modern hypnotherapy. All of these arts used symbols to formalize their technology, and all of them were original products of the creative imagination.

In other words, they were derived originally from the use of intuition, filtered by rationale, just as my father taught me.

The Renaissance, that great fifteenth-century rebirth of learning, gave a unique opportunity to imaginative, but rational minds, like Leonardo da Vinci, to explore the wonders of Nature. He was a near-perfect combination of artist and scientist, in the sense of the wholeness of Renaissance man, of which Leonardo was the archetype.

During the course of his life he became a master of anatomical drawing, by his acute observation and painstaking dissections of both human and animal remains. He was also an expert engineer, architect and builder, as well as being a master-mason in stone, a sculptor, a gun and cannon maker, and a painter of world renown.

His sketchbooks are a revelation of his *foreknowledge* of the industrialized world to come and his inventions ranged from flying machines, diving helmets and submarine vessels, to armoured fighting vehicles, helicopters, machine-tools, drilling machines, lathes, and advanced weaponry on a scale previously undreamt of. Add to this Leonardo's skill in hydraulics, canal-building and the construction of great fortifications and you have a man of outstanding stature. This extraordinary person was also a fine musician, chemist, and scholar of all natural phenomena.

He was the embodiment of the word genius, yet he had never attended a university.

Leonardo da Vinci is the supreme example of the open-minded gnostic, for both art and science are the true reflections of the Gnosis, and as such are indissolubly linked.

They seem to me to have the same relationship that exists, as Einstein showed us, in the case of space and time. Those dimensions of existence are so completely inter-related and interdependent, that, *ipso facto*, they are virtually the same entity: *Space-Time*.

So it should be with the arts and the sciences.

To follow in Leonardo's footsteps, searchers after truth who attempt to find their way through the complexities of the endless maze of inner space, need to understand the nature of symbols, much like those used to mark the features on a large-scale map. Creativity and the full use of imagination require such directional signposts, otherwise the adventurous practitioners of this form of inner navigation quickly find themselves becoming disorientated, and are soon lost.

For a safe journey into the inner space of the human imagination, immediately recognizable symbols are required by the infranaut, in the same way that the astronaut uses astrophysics and three-dimensional astro-navigation, to find a safe path through the infinity of outer space, where also there is no up nor down, no north, south, east, nor west.

Without the equivalent knowledge of the physics of the mind, a mentally unprepared voyage into the abyss of the unconscious mind, often, tragically, leads to disaster. This is why religious bodies, and many modern psychologists, give such solemn warnings of dire peril to the human mind, or soul, should a person seek to dabble in the occult.

All of which is perfectly sensible.

What is missing from that fearsome caveat are the words: 'Without proper training and knowledge of the powerful forces at work within the unconscious mind.'

Therefore, to combine such a journey into inner space with the use of any sort of drug, which, whether hard or soft, affects the mind, is an open invitation to a nervous breakdown, insanity, or even physical death.

I am not overstating the case!

I completely disagree with Doctor Timothy Leary, the American psychiatrist, and others whose over-liberal attitude towards drugs affected a generation of young people by, apparently, advocating the use of such mind-bending alkaloids.

That is why my father took such a long time and so much care to train me, while continually emphasizing the dangers of the misuse of any kind of drug, which could affect the mind.

His advice bears repetition:

'Never go on a mental voyage unprepared. Always use a focus, to determine the direction of your thinking. Always plan your return route and give yourself a time-limit for your mental journey.

'Never undertake such a journey when fatigued, unwell, or under the influence of alcohol, or mind-disorientating drugs.

'Until you have mastered a safe technique for inner navigation, never make such a journey alone. Always have a trusted watcher beside you, to see that you return safely to your body.'

It all sounds somewhat melodramatic but, I assure you, those words are full of wisdom. They are the basis of safe mental navigation through the trackless, wonderful worlds of the imagination.

The arcane Jewish art of the Cabala encapsulates such knowledge and reduces it to a series of techniques, teaching the art of safe navigation among the dangers of inner space. Sadly, much of the Cabala was written in a complex encyphered form during the thirteenth century, to protect its original authors, who were rabbis, from the Inquisition of those perilous times.

Therefore, it is hard, even for an adept Hebrew scholar, to unravel all of this document's deliberately obscured knowledge. The Cabala was, traditionally, passed down by word of mouth to a chosen few and before the thirteenth century, it was never written down, in order to protect its secrets from the profane.

Since the days of the Inquisition, much has been written about this basically simple chart to inner space, which further complicates its principles and generates even more obscure versions of its truth, placing it firmly in the category of mumbo-jumbo.

I often wonder if the Cabala was the basis from which the game of 'Snakes and Ladders' originated, in which the players laboriously climb the ladders or, involuntarily, slide back down the snakes, as a reminder of a mind-technique long forgotten, except by the few dedicated researchers who still pursue its fascinating teachings.

The study of Kabalism, as it is sometimes known, is really the province of the qualified rabbinical scholar, who soon weeds out the obscurities from the text, but a number of excellent works have been written by genuine researchers, like William Gray and Violet Firth (who wrote under the pseudonym of Dion Fortune).

Having said that, let me add that a study of the Cabala is not for the nervous or the weak-minded, as it offers no easy path to knowledge of yourself, and requires a dedication and determined scholarship, which might lead certain people into the pitfalls of obsession, and subsequent possession.

Here is yet another reason for using the safety-valve of your commonsense, and this certainly applies to the study of the Cabala. Moreover, the rules that my father specified are equally applicable to *all* meditative techniques.

First, you must learn to train your imagination to work in the medium of creative thought which most suits you. This could be pictorial, audio-visual, musical, conceptual (with or without concrete form), emotional, in words or three-dimensional shapes, or whatever method and type of thinking you find to be the most comfortable for your mind.

As I am mainly a pictorial and three-dimensional thinker, in concrete forms, apart from dialogue (which I seem to hear, clairaudiently), let me start with the development of the imagination along these lines.

However, the same safety rules apply, no matter what medium of thought comes to you most naturally. In other words, whether you are an artist, scientist, sculptor or musician, philosopher, engineer, mathematician, physicist, chemist, or just a straightforward seeker after truth, the method of developing your imagination should be, approximately, the same.

The only safe way is to proceed slowly and methodically, without overtaxing, or overtiring your mind. The Tibetan Lamas call this way: 'The Long Path'. When my father started me on this endless road, he made me relax and wind down my thinking process, until I felt comfortable and free from tension.

Pop explained why he did this, as closely as I can recall his words: 'The mind cannot think imaginatively, if it is under too much stress.

'Deadlines, as we have come to accept them in our modern, commercial world, do not exist for the creative mind, which can and will operate only at the pace that each individual thinker finds most comfortable. An overtense mind will not function at full efficiency, especially if the deadlines of the material world intrude, or interfere with its full freedom of operation.'

Once Pop got my mind to slow down from its habitual whirl of undisciplined thoughts, I could relax and allow the material world to fade into the background.

He then proceeded to the next lesson, which was: 'How to focus the mind into a definite channel of thought.'

At first, we used basic symbols as the focus, like those found on Zenner cards, which are often employed in experiments with telepathy. These cards are named after their inventor, Doctor Zenner, and were used by Doctor Rhine, at Duke University, Carolina, during his researches into ESP (extrasensory perception), mind-reading, telekinesis and other forms of paranormal phenomena.

Basically, these are forms and shapes, such as the square, triangle, circle, crescent, and cross, etc., set against a contrasting white background.

The object of these exercises is to concentrate, without blinking, on each individual shape, for about a minute, or until the outline of the shape appears to flash or shimmer, and then to transfer your gaze to a target surface of a different, contrasting colour. This technique was referred to as the Flashing Colours by members of the Golden Dawn (the turn-of-the-century ritual group of scholarly magicians, such as Aleister Crowley).

Immediately, because of the ability of the human eye to retain an image on its sensitive area, called the retina, which lines the back of the eyeball like a cinema screen, the viewer will see an image of the same shape, but in a different complementary colour, apparently projected on to the target surface.

So far, there is nothing paranormal or unscientific about this mental exercise, as it is a natural physiological process.

However, after several sessions of concentrated viewing of these basic shapes, which were called Tattvas by the Ancients, my father directed me to project them on to the neutrally-coloured target surface, but this time, *without* first gazing at them. In other words, he told me to conjure up the same images *solely* by the use of my memory.

To my surprise, I found I could do this quite easily.

Pop told me that some Japanese artists, who specialize in naturalistic painting, use the same technique in their art. However, instead of dividing the artists' attention, by constantly referring back to the subject, say a chicken, and then transferring its image on to the paper, bit by bit, as a Western painter would do, the Oriental artists fix their gaze *exclusively* on the fowl. Only after a long period of intense concentration, in which every detail has become imprinted on the painters' unconscious mind, will the artists finally shift their attention to the paper. Then, with a few strokes of the brush, the painters quickly draw the bird, with adept skill and an extraordinary attention to detail. Having seen a number of these beautiful paintings, which are full of life, I can appreciate the immense skill and mental discipline involved.

From these early experiments with the Tattvas, my father encouraged me to use more complex shapes and forms, starting with a combination of the basic Zenner cards, but this time superimposing several different shapes, *simultaneously*.

I also found this to be quite easy, projecting the combined images on to a light-coloured background, which I used as the target surface.

Now it was time to try something harder, and I would concentrate on a scene, usually a picture-postcard view of some part of the world with which I was unfamiliar, such as an Italian village set on the shores of a lake. For these sessions, I would gaze rather longer on the picture before projecting the miniature scene on to the target surface, which in this case was a white wall.

After several successful attempts at these mental projections, which, of course, were seen on the wall in different colours to the ones on the picture-postcard, Pop would let me rest for a few minutes and then ask me to conjure up the same scene, this time *without* referring back to the picture.

This test of my pictorial memory worked remarkably well and improved with each successive exercise, and, in these cases, the colours remained the *same* as the ones on the pictures.

It was an excellent way to train my developing imagination, for, after a few attempts, I could conjure up and project the same scene, without the usual period of prolonged concentration, because the image had sunk so deeply into my unconscious mind.

This, of course, was a deliberately-induced illusion.

However, I found it tiring and my father rationed these visualization sessions to the minimum time required to establish this unusual technique.

From then on, it was only a question of practice before I could integrate a whole scene from various *different* images, in the same way that artists make up their finished paintings out of a number of diverse elements, which they have drawn previously in their sketchbooks. The only difference was that I was using a mental sketchbook to jot down the various images in my memory.

Apparently, this was much the same imaginative technique as the one used by the great Serbo-Croatian electrical-engineer, Nikola Tesla, the inventor of the alternating-current and polyphase-current induction motors, turbo-electric generators and many other patented inventions that gave the world power and light and ushered in the Age of Electricity.

This man's extraordinary genius for invention and creative thought was studiously ignored, after he annoyed the scientific Establishment in 1912 by refusing the Nobel Prize. Actually, he objected to *sharing* the prize with Thomas Edison, for whom he once had worked, because Tesla had done all the original mathematical calculations for the alternating-current induction motors, while Edison was the inventor of the much more primitive direct-current induction motor, with its limited range of about a quarter of a mile.

Of course, Tesla was right, because Edison was not a scientist and had little knowledge of mathematics, being more an inventive super-salesman rather than a qualified engineer, but the Establishment never forgave Tesla and virtually wiped him out from their scientific history books.

Therefore, the credit for these revolutionary inventions in the generation of power and light was given to George Westinghouse, to whom Tesla had sold his patents. Furthermore, in a quixotic moment of generosity, Tesla had refused to accept any royalties which would have accrued to him. Just imagine what those royalties would have been worth. They would have made Tesla as Midas-rich as Westinghouse soon became.

The great Serbian genius died alone and nearly penniless, in a small apartment, situated at the top of a New York hotel building owned by Westinghouse. At least, the man who had bought Tesla's patent rights didn't charge him rent.

I have copies of all the inventions which Tesla copyrighted, issued by the US Patent Office, and I have no doubt that this story is true.

So amazingly well could this extraordinary man's creative mind wield his imagination, that Tesla only drew detailed plans of his complex machinery *after* they had been built. Many of these rough sketches in his own hand are to be found in his fascinating diaries, yet these contained all the exact measurements, which were accurate to an Angstrom (one ten billionth of a metre).

There were plenty of witnesses to Tesla's extraordinary inner-vision, because he would often describe his amazing machines to friends, like Samuel Clements (Mark Twain), in complete detail, long before he had built them and tried them out.

An amusing story of one of the great American humorist's visits to Tesla's laboratory in New York, illustrates the power of the Serbian inventor's machines.

Apparently, Mark Twain had been warned by Tesla not to sit for too long on a certain chair, which was placed over a powerful low-frequency electrical generator. Twain did not believe his friend's warning and challenged Tesla to switch on the machine, to full power.

The inventor, who had a rather strange sense of humour, was well aware of the unpleasant side-effect that this oscillator produced, but he accepted the challenge and threw the switch.

Mark Twain sat, smiling and smoking a cigar, while the gently vibrating chair built up to full power. Then, suddenly, his expression changed to one of alarm, and the famous author made a frantic rush for the toilet. He reached it, just in time.

The effect of the powerful low-frequency oscillations had loosened his bowels.

Genius is never a popular trait, because it generally makes those in authority feel inadequate and, therefore, threatened.

Minds like Nikola Tesla's are all too rare and, as was the case with Albert Einstein, such geniuses at first are derided, until they come up with an idea from which a fortune can be made.

Then, astute business people set about robbing them, if they can, or, alternatively, using them for their own ends, if they cannot actually steal their ideas. The usual excuse is, of course: 'There is no copyright in an *idea*!'

I am certainly no genius, but I am an original thinker, within the terms that I have already defined, and I have suffered from plagiarism for most of my working life. So, I believe I know a little of what Tesla must have felt at his massive betrayal.

Fortunately, original thinkers now can do something about this intolerable situation which has been going on far too long in Britain, and in many other parts of the world, because, at the present time, these unscrupulous practices, at last, are being brought out into the open.

Please don't make the same mistakes that I made, of trusting to a so-called gentleman's agreement. Get it in writing, in triplicate, and properly attested, no matter how well established or reputable the organization that you are dealing with may be.

By 1936, at the end of two years' training at home, with my father, and a few extra sessions working with approved mediums, who were trusted friends, I had become proficient enough to be able to project my mind, at will, into the boundless realms of my imagination.

I now held the key to unlock my unconscious mind, any time I wished to do so. However, I also had learnt to ration these free-scanning mental trips so that they did not overtax my energy, as I was growing-up at that time, and this was of prime importance, because puberty uses up a lot of energy.

This ignorance of the importance of control in developing the creative mind, and the consequent profligacy in the use of a creative person's imagination, may be one explanation why a genius, like Mozart, died at such an early age. Besides him, there are many examples of artists and scientists, both male and female, with highly creative minds living comparatively short lives, probably due to this same lack of control, and the attendant overtaxing of their physical health.

What did I gain from all these training sessions?

In practical terms, I developed the ability to think in an original way, which is the main reason why, to my surprise, I can still earn my living, at the age of sixty-six.

That is not the boasting of a wealthy man, which I certainly am not. Nor is it the big-headed arrogance of some overnight star in show business. I am well aware of that human frailty, which so often suddenly attacks successful writers and performers, many of them the synthetic products of today's skilful publicists, backed by the technical brilliance and the power of the media.

It is simply a statement of fact.

Even though I have been informed that practically all my many original recordings, spanning at least ten years, both in TV and radio, have been wiped, on the orders of some BBC official, I am grateful that I am still remembered by many of the viewers and listeners who enjoyed my past work.

That is a tremendous plus, but it doesn't compensate for the loss of large potential earnings in the media, now being enjoyed by others, some of whom copied, or recognizably based their comedy on my original work.

If I am wrong, and those many recordings of my TV and radio shows, such as *It's a Square World*, and my years of work on the *Goon Show*, still exist, then will the networks involved in their recording please produce them.

Fortunately, my children's shows still exist. In the case of the *Bumblies*, which are happily remembered by many of the generation who saw them over thirty years ago, in 1954-5, this is solely because I made these films privately, and therefore still own the negatives.

Michael Bentine's Potty Time, my other children's show, of which I made some seventy programmes for the commercial network, is still played in many parts of the world, due to the foresight of my good friend, Muir Sutherland, who persuaded Thames Television to buy them outright. This series alone earns me much goodwill in my travels round the world. Sadly, only memories of the others remain, but they still prompt people, whom I have never met before, to stop me and say: 'I just wanted to say "thank you", for all the enjoyment you have given me and my family, over the years.'

That, for me, is a wonderful reward for all the hard work I put into those shows, but, unfortunately, it does not help to pay the bills. In fact I am the only founder member of the *Goon Show* who has had no residual payment for all my pioneering work.

Once again, I mention these facts to point out how the misuse of petty authority can destroy many years of hard work. That is something that the creative person must beware of and learn to avoid, if the just rewards of his or her original thinking, worry and exhausting effort are to be harvested from the Establishment. I assure you that the experience can be heartbreaking.

From the age of thirteen, those early lessons with my father stood me in good stead by widening my horizons, thereby giving me the ability to absorb knowledge like a sponge.

I believe this was because I could now retain the written word, in the form of pictorial images that my reading conjured up for me. This is what so-called photographic memory is all about, and this ability can, demonstrably, be trained and sharpened to an extraordinary degree.

At least, in my own case this has proven to be so, and I am sure that, if an imaginative reader follows the instructions in this book, he or she may well be able to do the same, and, very probably, much better.

It all depends on how you go about it.

Once you have mastered the techniques of controlling your thoughts and learnt how to project your mind into the realms of creative imagination, the rest is a matter of sensibly-rationed practice and self-discipline.

It is entirely up to you!

It may not come easily, at first. You have to learn to accept that fact and keep trying, but the more relaxed you become when performing these exercises, the better.

Probably, one of the first adventures into the imagination that you will undertake will be the flying-dream. This is often an involuntary experience during normal sleep and can be both delightful and exhilarating, as you swoop low over the visualized landscape, skimming along, following the contours of the changing scene, to land light as a bird at the end of the flight and wake up safely in your bed.

The whole process is not unlike that of the flight, which you can enjoy on the ground, in a modern aircraft-simulator, or when playing with similar software on a home computer, except that, in a flying-dream you become *part* of the actual simulation, rather than just watching the action on a TV monitor.

How different is the falling-dream, which usually occurs with those who suffer from vertigo. This built-in fear of high places is often expressed in the form of a dream-fall from a great height, with the sleeper feeling the sensation of tumbling towards the ground and only waking up when about to hit bottom.

It is a most unpleasant experience!

A popular fallacy is that the bump that you feel at the end of this short dream sequence is caused by your heart restarting after missing a beat, presumably due to the fear of the sensation of falling, which is horribly real.

However, the true flying-dream, which can be duplicated by those whose imagination has been well-trained, is one of the most rewarding of all the out-of-the-body-experiences.

It is often synthesized by those enthusiasts who build model airplanes, especially when they fly them by radio-control. The sensation of such a transferred experience is so vivid, that these model-aircraft buffs habitually tell you of their flights, as though they themselves had been in the cockpit of the model plane. It is an excellent example of the joy of using the imagination, to enact wish-fulfilment.

When your mental projection has become easily controllable, in duration as well as directionally, the extent of these OOBEs can be increased safely, but, at first, it is a wise precaution to have a trusted watcher beside you, just in case you come up against a dream-experience which unduly distresses you.

In that case your friend, with a few stroking passes of his or her hands through the aura surrounding your body, can wipe away the disturbing condition (which is, by its very nature, electro-chemically induced) and safely return you to consciousness, without distress or shock.

There is no mumbo-jumbo involved. We are simply discussing straightforward electrical interference, by one electro-chemical generator interacting with another.

In its essence this soothing action is similar to that of a mother comforting a frightened child after a nightmare, or arousing a sleep-walker, without shocking them harmfully awake. Obviously, in either of those cases, gentleness and a relaxed, but positive attitude is indicated. The same sympathetic approach by the watcher, combined with the wiping away of the disturbed aura can be regarded as standard operating procedure, when practising OOBEs.

It was only after a lot of dual instruction from my father, who sat patiently beside me, while I left my body in his care, that he finally allowed me to go solo, in the terms of an out-of-the-body- experience.

As Pop was an aeronautical engineer, aircraft and aerodynamics were very much a part of my childhood, so the terminology of the aircraft industry, of which my father had been an early and effective pioneer, was as familiar to me as schoolboy slang.

Recently, I was presented, by the Royal Aeronautical Establishment at Farnborough, with one of Pop's early inventions. This was a Tensometer, for gauging the stresses and strains on wire-braced aircraft, which my father had made, to obviate the handicap of tone deafness, from which he suffered, at the time when the all-important bracing-wires of these aircraft were tensioned by using tuning-forks.

In Pop's own words: 'I only knew it was the National Anthem that the orchestra was playing, when people stood up!'

Typically, my father gave his inventions to the RAeE, to be used for the furtherance of safety in flight. It was very heart-warming that this splendid part of the Establishment had not forgotten Pop's unselfish gesture.

My father had been a budding electrical and mechanical engineer when news of the Wright brothers' epoch-making flight burst on the world.

'Typical Yankee exaggeration!' was the first British reaction, when the news came of that historic hop of a few airborne yards.

But Pop became fired with a determination to be part of this new Age of Flight and quickly adapted his knowledge of mathematics and heavy engineering to the problems of ultra-light aerodynamics. In a few years, my father had spanned the yawning gap between locomotives, giant A/C generators and dynamos, and the lightweight flying-machines of the pre-1914 era.

Almost to the day of his death, Pop would look up at the sound of an aeroplane.

How often he told me: 'If they don't look right, they don't fly right!'

So, for me, it was hardly a surprise that some of my first experiences of mind projection should be in the form of flying-dreams.

CHAPTER FOUR

We have lift-off

You are soon going to be faced with the next big step in going solo, having prepared yourselves as best you can. In the RAF the student pilot was washed-out if, after flying dual with an instructor for a set number of hours, he failed to fly solo and demonstrate his mastery of the machine.

Allowing for a certain amount of flexibility in the interpretation of this principle, similar rules should apply to the training of a student infranaut. If it is obvious that too much distress is being experienced by the fledgling testing the wings of the mind, an immediate return to the body and a period of retraining is indicated, before he or she can be allowed to go solo, safely.

In the wartime RAF, when the need for trained aircrew forced the pace of flying-training to the danger point, I found myself facing the need to brief one young Lancaster bomber crew, whose pilot had a total of 120 hours flying time, including *one night-time cross-country flight.*

The whole crew were all brand new sergeants, and their average age was eighteen.

That baby-faced aircrew was the epitome of the pre-war flying films of the thirties, like the *Dawn Patrol*, where the grizzled veteran looks in disgusted horror at the half-trained youngsters he now has to send to almost certain death.

My father told me that, by 1917, boy-pilots were being sent into battle with insufficient training, and were often unable to cope with adverse weather conditions, so that more of them were killed in flying accidents than by the enemy fighters.

In 1943, I had to pass as 'Fit for operational flying' youngsters who had barely managed to find the airfield in bad weather. If I remember correctly, that particular crew lasted one operation. I often wonder whether they even found the target, a heavily defended city in the industrial Ruhr.

My protests were backed up by my senior Intelligence Officer, a veteran pilot of the 1914-18 war. They fell on deaf ears, and the CO, an insensitive career-officer, ordered that eager teenage crew to fly on the next night's operation, from which, of course, they never returned. I don't think they even had time to unpack.

Nowadays, as it was before the Second World War, the modern student pilot in the RAF is allowed to progress to the next step in his flight-training, only after completely mastering each phase of his flying instruction. In view of the greatly increased complexity of modern aircraft, this cautious progressive training is the only answer to safe flying.

So it should be with OOBEs.

Fortunately, for our purposes, flying is confined to the mind, but, without adequate instruction and sensible precautions in allowing the student infranaut to progress at his or her natural rate, there can be much danger in ignoring those simple safety precautions, which my father outlined for me all those years ago.

You have all the time in the world to open your mind. So why rush it?

That is why I am deeply concerned by many of these high-powered seminars, which are being offered to those who are willing to part with large sums of money, to be trained by some self-styled guru, with a glib tongue, little knowledge, and no conscience whatsoever. When that same teacher recommends hallucinogenic drugs, as the quick way to the opening of the mind, I really get worried and long for some governmental sort of control. Sadly, this kind of Bunco operation, apparently, is not covered by that wise piece of legislation – the Trades Description Act – and any phoney Master can set up these seminars and charge extortionate rates for 'Awakening your Mind', or 'Helping you to walk among the Gods'. It is only when the illicit use of drugs is involved that the authorities can step in.

Beware of the quack guru.

Nowadays, phonies by the hundreds are starting to flock towards this rapidly expanding area of Awareness, which, at present, is being given far more exposure in the media than ever before.

The reason for this sudden interest in the opening of the mind is partly due to the approaching millennium, and the strange effect that this event seems to exert on people, even on those for whom this is not a millennium in the religious sense, that it is to the non-Christians of the world.

After all, this *is* only the Christian Millennium and applies to a comparatively small proportion of the world's population, even though Christians are numbered in hundreds of millions. For the bulk of the earth's huge population, the year 2000 of the Christian era does not apply!

Yet, strangely enough, similar disturbing effects and a sense of unease seem to apply almost as much to those who presumably should be indifferent to the mystical significance of the rapidly approaching millennium.

Why should this be so?

What does the word millennium mean?

It merely signifies the end of a thousand-year period: no more and no less!

Nevertheless, the psychological effect that it is having on a large proportion of the world's population is one reason why so many people, who, until recently, were quite content to leave their religious instruction in the hands of their church are now seeking other methods of opening their minds. This is probably in an attempt to find some other reason for existence, besides the gross materialism which so often seems to control their lives.

For example, in Russia, since the Revolution of 1916, the official religion, or political mind attitude of the Soviet Republics, has been atheism. But today a very large proportion of the people, who make up the Russian entity, which is composed of over a hundred different ethnic groups, each with its own language, openly or clandestinely, devoutly follow the religion of their ancestors which could be Christianity, Judaism, Buddhism, or the Muslim Faith, while Shamanism, the Earth-Magic of the tribal medicine-man, is still widely practised in Siberia and other remote parts of Soviet Russia.

Even Marxism and Communism, with their joint concept of the world brotherhood of man, and Dialectic Materialism are insufficient to fulfil the *spiritual needs of the people*.

It seems that there is much truth in the words: 'Man cannot live by bread alone.'

Furthermore, it is obvious, by the number of reports from Russia of a thriving research programme into the parameters of the paranormal, that there is growing Soviet support for this area of the exploration of the mind.

Recently, there has been an increasing tendency by the Soviets to classify such research projects under the general blanket of State Security. At the same time, Soviet scientists are exhibiting eagerness to find out how other countries' research programmes into the paranormal are progressing.

As my friend, Professor Eric Laithwaite said: 'If sufficient commercial applications for paranormal abilities, or their effective use in Defence or War could be found, the funds available for research into these areas of the mind would be limitless.'

In the last war, to my surprise, I found out from Intelligence sources, that both sides of the struggle were using propaganda methods employing the occult, to a considerable extent.

Propaganda ministries, both Allied and German, and especially the clandestine set-ups, like the British one at Bletchley Park, used the Quatrains or verses of Nostradamus, the famous seer of the sixteenth century, to angle their propaganda towards indications of coming victory, for whichever side was employing the long-dead prophet's predictions.

Astrology also was used extensively, by both Hitler and Heinrich Himmler, the head of the SS, to indicate the probable course of the war. In fact, both these madmen had teams of astrologers working for them.

The late Ewen Montagu, who wrote *The man who never was* and *Beyond Top Secret*, two excellent accounts of his involvement in the Second World War top secret Intelligence operations, told me that when he was a brand new assistant to Admiral Godfrey, the wartime Director of British Naval Intelligence, one of the first orders he received was to find three astrologers for his chief.

'Surely, sir, you don't believe in such things?' asked Ewen, puzzled by his commanding officer's odd request.

'No, I don't!' replied the Admiral. 'But Hitler and several of the top Nazis do. So hop out and bring me three of the best astrologers you can find, Montagu!'

'Did it work?' I asked my wise friend.

He grinned.

'Not really! I couldn't find two astrologers who agreed about the interpretation of their charts, let alone three!'

Apparently, the Admiralty also employed the dowsing (divining) talents of an elderly couple, who, presumably at Admiral Godfrey's request, regularly visited the Admiralty chart-room, which in wartime was reputed to be harder to get into than the kingdom of heaven.

There, once or twice a week, these experienced dowsers would use their pendulums, swung over top secret charts, to locate the position and trace the movements of enemy ships.

They must have had significant success, confirmed by the Photographic Reconnaissance Units of the RAF and Fleet Air Arm scouting planes, because this practice continued for a considerable time, until, evidently, the strain proved too much for the elderly couple and they had to desist.

Another interesting sidelight on the clandestine war was that Colonel Maxwell Knight, the wartime Head of MI5 (Counter-Espionage) was a close friend of Aleister Crowley, and was, himself, deeply interested in ritual-magic.

Dennis Wheatley, the famous author, and an acknowledged expert on ritual-magic, was part of Winston Churchill's wartime advisory staff. He acted as a synthesizer of possible Nazi schemes and plans for the invasion of Britain, Gibraltar, Africa and other probable targets.

A sub-lieutenant in the First World War, Wheatley was quickly promoted to the rank of Wing-Commander and sat in on many of Churchill's top secret conferences, writing and submitting reports and scenarios for Hitler's possible alternative plans. One wonders on what other aspects of the Nazis and their dark obscenities Dennis Wheatley, as an expert on the occult, with an extensive library of rare books on that subject, advised Winston Churchill and his wartime team.

Long after the war, when he kindly invited me to his flat in Sloane Street, and we discussed these matters, he would only hint at the real purposes of his wartime job. One thing clearly emerged from my meeting with that delightful and interesting man. The knowledgeable author was deeply concerned about the sudden upsurge and misuse of the occult and Black Magic, in our present times.

So with due apologies for my attitude of doom and gloom about too-precipitate a launching into the realms of inner space, let us now take the next step: a cautious solo flight. Still using RAF parlance, this is to be a Circuit and Bump.

71

Sitting, or lying, comfortably relaxed in a favourite chair, on a sofa or bed, you are going to let your mind leave your body and roam round a specific target.

Let us choose, for this flight of fancy, a focus such as the one I used over fifty-five years ago: a picture of a village in Europe.

Concentrate on the picture, to the exclusion of all other thoughts.

Let your mind enter the scene.

Closely examine every detail of the picture.

Try to visualize what it is like inside the houses, and what lies behind them, hidden from view.

Immerse yourself in the whole scene.

Now, close your eyes and continue to visualize the scene in every detail, wandering through it in your mind as though you were physically there.

Once again, with your eyes open, carefully note the colours of the flowers and the shape, form and texture of the buildings, the formations of the clouds in the sky, and the outline and shape of the trees on the horizon. If there is a lake, or the scene is of a seaside village, listen with your mind to the lapping of the water. Visualize what is going on out there on the horizon, and even beyond it. See if there are boats moving across the face of the waters, and imagine yourself aboard them.

Let yourself become totally absorbed into the scene, until you feel its reality, for it is, after all, a reflection of an actual place, which you could physically visit. Close your eyes and try to recall every detail. If your concentration weakens, come back out of the scene and start again, with the same procedures, but do *not* continue to do so, if you feel yourself becoming tired.

Finally with your eyes open make the mental effort to withdraw yourself from the scene, until you visualize it, once more, as just a picture in a book.

If you think this is all airy-fairy nonsense and pointless, remember how you feel when you are reading a well-written thriller; how you can be completely absorbed in the story, so that you are swept along by the excitement being generated by the book.

Hence the expression: 'Once I picked up the book, I couldn't put it down.'

For a time, possibly even for hours on end, you become a part of the book, but if there is an interruption, often to your annoyance, you find yourself back in the room, just reading words printed on a page, and nothing more. After you have dealt with the interruption, it may take you a few minutes before you refocus your mind on the words and get back into the story. We have all experienced that situation many times, and yet we never consider how strange it is.

Many of us also have studied drawings by Escher, that fine draughtsman and geometer who specializes in devising intricate pictures, in which optical illusions become apparent.

It takes quite an effort of will to orientate the mind while studying one of his fascinating pictures. Stairways that should point upwards suddenly point downwards, outside walls become inside ones and the whole world of Escher's creations become topsy-turvy, if you allow them to do so. His work is really mind-boggling in its ever-changing illusions.

The same sort of sequence of events and instantly changing perspectives can often occur in a dream, from which we wake and then try hard to fall back to sleep to continue to view the fascinating dreamscape from where we left off.

I'm sure we all have had that happen to us, especially when the dream is a particularly pleasant one.

On your concentrated mental journey, or controlled daydream, if that is how you prefer to think of it, you are of course consciously writing your own scenario, deliberately guiding your mind deep into the realms of the imagination, just as your favourite authors have done in the books which took you along with them on their imaginary journeys.

This is what Daniel Defoe described as his voyages in a paper boat.

All this talk of precautions and prayers, careful preparations and disciplined mental drills may seem to be a ridiculous melodramatization of this whole business. But I assure you, this cautious attitude of mind is necessary because the imaginative mind is a sensitive instrument and can become deeply disturbed, if it is not being properly controlled.

For example, how many of us, with vivid imaginations, have been ill-advised or incautious enough to read a ghost story, by those masters of the horror genre, M. R. James, Algernon Blackwood, Peter Straub, Howard Lovecraft, Bram Stoker and Stephen King, late at night in an empty house, and become so absorbed in the pervasive sense of horror, that, sleepless and shivering with fear, we have longed for the comfort of the dawn.

I'm sure many of us have done that.

But, at least, in those cases we could always tell ourselves that it was *only* a story in a book that was giving us the waking nightmare.

Imagine how it would be, if you could not reason with yourself along those comforting lines, but instead, found yourself unable to wake out of a terrifying nightmare world of *your own* creation.

That is not a nice thought!

Another disturbing aspect of an uncontrolled imagination which frequently occurs, especially among more emotional Latin people, is when tragedy strikes as a result of insane jealousy taking control of an over-imaginative lover.

I call this the Othello Syndrome.

How many *crimes passionelles* have been committed, due to false rumours and the inflamed imagination of jealous lovers? These often lead to gunshots or fatal stab wounds and the death of one or more of the objects of such jealousy, as well as frequently ending in the suicide of the demented homicidal lover.

74

Terror, sometimes induced by some imaginary peril, can cause a fatal heart attack, or apoplexy, and there are many unexplained cases of people being found dead for no immediately apparent cause, but who have been known to be dabblers in the occult.

So I really do mean what I say, when emphasizing how easy it is for a nervous person, with a highly-strung temperament and an over-active, uncontrolled imagination to find themselves in bad trouble.

That is why I chose the peaceful book illustration, as an ideal focus for the first solo flight of a newly-opened mind.

Several of these controlled mental excursions into the detailed background of an ordinary book illustration, or a picture postcard, should prepare you for the next stage of your mental flight-training.

This time, the focus for your journey is to be a *fictional* book illustration, not a photograph of an *actual* place. For example, choose a picture of an Ancient Egyptian Temple, as it was believed to have been at the time of the dynasties of the Middle Kingdom, or a reconstruction of the palace of King Minos, at Knossos in Crete, long before the Christian era.

Note that both these fictitious paintings are archetypal, and that I, deliberately, have not chosen a scene of violence, such as the 'Tortures of the Spanish Inquisition', 'Trafalgar', or 'The Battle of the Somme', or some horrific overview of the recent Holocaust. Obviously scenes of violent and bloody action are not a good idea for the target of an early OOBE. All too quickly they can become deeply disturbing, disorientating, and dangerously traumatic, especially for a young person, and this is why I am so concerned about all the *gratuitous* violence on television.

I sincerely believe that the alarming rise in violent and sadistic crimes of the most ghastly kind has been triggered by the constant exposure on television of too much explicit cruelty, involving the deliberate infliction of pain and suffering on helpless victims, in far too many horror films.

There is strong evidence that the recent appalling mass murder at Hungerford, in which fourteen innocent people were slaughtered by a crazed young British gunman, was one such dreadful result of too much TV and movie screen violence.

In this case the authorities reacted quickly, by curbing the supply of such deadly weapons as semi-automatic assault rifles to the legitimate holders of firearms certificates, but nothing has been done, so far, to limit the increasing transmission of this genre of mindless horror programmes that tend to initiate such acts of sadistic terror.

In fact, some television current affairs and news programmes actually generate a romantic mystique surrounding hijackers of aircraft and other terrorist thugs engaged in murderous acts of international piracy, calling them by the name of 'Freedom Fighters'.

Certainly this is one of the apparent dangers inherent in exposing young minds to explicit scenes of violence and sudden death. Pictorial settings of violence are clearly undesirable for these intense sessions of mental projection, hence the deliberate choice of peaceful subjects for these flights of fancy.

Having chosen an appropriate fictional scene to explore, go through the same procedures as before, but this time imagine the scene as though it were *not* fictional. Proceed to enter the scene exactly as before, circling behind the two-dimensional presentation of the picture, and imagining yourself at the rear of the buildings or background scenery.

This time also imagine the people who would have lived in those remote times, and, if the picture does not have figures in the scene, create your own.

You can do this by having previously concentrated on pictures of people of the times and then inserting them into the scene, just as I did with the different images of

Zenner cards, which I overlaid on each other, during my earliest mind-exercises. Alternatively, you can make up your own characters. It all depends on how imaginative you are becoming.

The whole object of these intensive mental exercises is to *gradually* stretch the imagination, and to *gently* widen the spectrum of creative thought.

Let me give you an example of how far-ranging these mental projections can be; in the nineteen-thirties, we employed a young girl called Florrie who helped Mother run the house. I believe she was part-gypsy and she had a great gift for this kind of OOBE.

I was present when, with her permission, Pop and a medical friend, who was a hypnotherapist, placed Florrie into a deep cataleptic trance, in which we could support her rigid body between two chairs, with her neck on one chair and her heels on the other. At no other point was her body supported!

This bright and cheerful girl, who was in a deep trance, felt no ill-effects whatsoever, even when I tentatively sat on her tummy, without my 100 pounds weight (at that time) having any apparent effect on her rigid body.

Of course my father and his medical friend did not leave her for longer than a half-a-minute or so in that extraordinary position, but made her relax in a comfortable armchair for the actual OOBE or astral travelling, as it was called in those days. My mother was also present, to act as a further witness and to fill the role of chaperone and I remember how amazed she was by the range of Florrie's flights into the astral plane.

Under these test conditions, which lasted for about twenty minutes, our pretty young friend would proceed to leave her body, watched attentively for any sign of distress by both my father and mother, and, following the instructions of the medical hypnotist, would 'travel' wherever she was directed to go.

I remember that one of these trips was to Chillham Castle, where the Ching family, who were friends of ours and who were interested in the paranormal, had their home.

Florrie was instructed to enter the castle and go upstairs, there to enter Mrs Ching's bedroom and describe the layout of the room.

During the OOBE the deeply-entranced girl was able to describe the whole of the castle bedroom, quite accurately.

All this was then confirmed, on the telephone, by a member of the Ching family, who also corroborated the fact that Florrie had never visited their castle, let alone ever been inside Mrs Ching's bedroom.

For me, this was a remarkable demonstration of the validity of astral travelling (or remote viewing), under hypnosis.

During my early training, under my father's instruction, after I had spent considerable time on these carefully graduated solo mental exercises, I used to bicycle out into the Kent countryside and sit for hours on the grass-covered chalk escarpment, overlooking the Romney Marsh.

This magical place had been drained by the Romans and I used to imagine the passing parade of Roman legions on the march along the spine of the South Downs. At Ham Street, an old Roman road, set high above the marsh, I also visualized medieval pilgrims, *en route* for Canterbury, or knights and squires, riding hard to catch the ship to take them to Calais and the Hundred Years War, and even eighteenth-century smugglers with grim revenuers in hot pursuit.

I often passed those long lazy summer holidays imagining the broad spectrum of all the other previous inhabitants of that historic part of Britain. For the Downland, with its organic chalk sub-structure, is ideal for storing four-dimensional images of its rich historical past, ready for the sensitive minds of the young to unlock its secrets.

It was a wonderful experience and a great exercise for my young mind. I thoroughly enjoyed that part of my boyhood and early youth, and I enthusiastically made these romantic and exciting creative journeys into my rapidly developing imagination.

I appreciated them even more, because I could now control my thoughts and direct them wherever I wanted to go and return safely to my body, any time I wished. I was in complete control, and, even when darkness fell, I felt no sense of unease.

During my teenage years I was a lonely boy, because I was so desperately shy – mainly because of my appalling stammer – although eventually it was cured; but this was my wonderful secret world and I could enter it, or leave it, safely, at will.

Not far from where I was pursuing my imaginative adventures in the timeless realms of creative thought, I knew that Rudyard Kipling had brought up his children, at Burwash, with much the same strong awareness of the romantic background of the Romney Marsh. Below me, as I sat on the rolling slopes of the Downs, I could see the ancient Cinque Port of Rye, where Henry James wrote his wonderful books. For me, it was truly a time of magic, all too soon to be lost in the dark thunderclouds of war which, like many other youngsters, I could sense approaching.

Allowing for the differences in basic thinking, this cautious approach to entering the imagination can be used by poets, writers, painters, architects, engineers, actors, musicians, mathematicians and even by purely abstract thinkers, with equal facility, once these simple principles have been mastered. However, it will be of little use to those who have *no* imagination and who think only within the confining parameters of personal recall and experience, without being able to use them as the basic building blocks of the mind.

It will be a waste of time if they cannot imagine *original* pictures, new three-dimensional shapes and forms in sculpture, or radical departures from contemporary architecture, different sound-patterns in musical composition, inventive mathematical or symbolic statements, or other revolutionary concepts in pure thought.

All these types of creative thinking are only within the reach of opened minds, and the further the horizon of the imagination is stretched and widened, the more flexible and inventive becomes their intuition. Therefore, the more adventurous these journeys into the continuum of the creative imagination become, the greater are the opportunities for acquiring new and wonderful experiences.

The result is that the mind retains ever more new building blocks, with which to improvise its creations, no matter what medium of thought is being used by the individual.

Once the imagination is stimulated into action, often by reading the classics and other well-written books, or by studying the works of great scientists, the rest is an on-going and ever-expanding process.

That is why the whole operation must be based on sound and safe principles in creative thinking. Otherwise, the state of mind soon becomes chaotic, leading to disorientation, irrational thinking, confusion, panic, and, eventually, insanity. This also is why the wise philosophers and alchemists of the past called this process of learning the Great Work, and laid down a strict regime, aimed at the safe development of the mental capabilities of their disciples.

To accomplish anything worthwhile takes a long time, and to rush things only results in avoidable accidents, unprofessional conduct and wasted time. Therefore, these imaginative exercises, which are designed to widen the scope of the creative mind, should be practised again and again, until they become second nature to the practitioner. That is how my father helped me to develop my imagination, and I will always be grateful to him for the painstaking care with which he guided me into the wonderful worlds of infinite thought.

When I read the *Sacred Magic of Abra-Melin, the Mage*, in the Macgregor Mathers' translation from the ancient French document, in the *Bibliothèque Arsenal* in Paris, I marvelled at the long and dedicated, preliminary conditioning process that the student ritual-magician had to undergo, before attempting to practise this effective method of ritual-magic, which is designed for the application of the power of the will.

Since then, I have known several good minds who have failed to survive this perilous course in applied will-power, without mental damage, solely because they failed to carry out the *full* six-month period of ritual conditioning and strict self-denial, which must precede it.

I believe that this conditioning process is not unlike the Spiritual Exercises devised by Ignatius Loyola, when he founded the Jesuit Order. Certainly, the rigid discipline of the six-month regime of fasting and prayer, meditation and mind-control, as required by the would-be practitioner of Abra-Melin ritual-magic needs a dedication that will test every ounce of will-power possessed by the apprentice magician.

Among other things, it requires the construction and scrupulously clean maintenance of an oratory, or dedicated place for uninterrupted solitary contemplation; meticulous personal cleanliness and total abstinence from sexual practices; as well as the religious performance of concentrated sessions of prayer at dawn, noon, dusk, and midnight throughout the full six-month vigil.

Even allowing for the great difference in life-styles of the past, both now and at the time the author of this work wrote as 'Abraham the Jew', it is time to say that *unless* the practitioner undergoes these demanding and dedicated preliminaries, as outlined in the book, he, or she, will be in grave danger of serious psychological damage.

Conversely, I truly believe that someone, who has the stamina and the right qualifications, in age and good health, both mentally and physically, to carry out that long period of self-denial and self-discipline, would benefit greatly from that strict mental and physical regime, and, in the words of one scholar, who had managed to stay the course of that strange apprenticeship: 'Such a person would be capable of entering the Gates of Hell itself, and could emerge, unscathed, having travelled among the realms of Evil and safely passed through the ranks of the Legions of Demons that guard the Satanic Inferno.'

That probably sounds overly melodramatic, but I assure you that the realms of the collective unconscious can harbour archetypal perils and monstrous creations of the mind. I know, for certain, that I am not one of those rare persons, able to carry out such a daunting quest. The acquisition of power does not interest me.

The simple and sensible exercises which I practised in my long period of training and the ones that I recommend for opening the mind, are nowhere near as demanding and are all reasonably easy to carry out. In practice, they only require a short time to devote yourself to them, during each training session, plus commonsense and a strong belief in their effectiveness.

All of which comes under the heading of applied faith.

These then are the simple instructions and flight regulations for your first solos into the collective unconscious, or, as I think of it, the realms of the universal overmind, taking you through the gates of the imagination by using the latent abilities of your unconscious mind.

To sum them up:

Preparation
Relaxation
Concentration
Projection
Investigation
Caution
And limitation by control, at all times!

Provided that these principles are adhered to and that a reliable watcher is there, beside you during your early attempts, until you are fully confident that you can handle these mental journeys alone, you should be quite safe. Furthermore, you should emerge from these trips into the creative imagination of inner space with much more awareness of yourself and the extraordinary abilities of your mind.

Moreover, you will never know whether these things are valid or not, until you experience them for yourself.

The situation, provided that you have been following these simple instructions, should be that you can do what I have done and leave your body, subjectively, or objectively, at will.

The difference between these two styles of mind-projection is that, with *objective* clairvoyance (clear-seeing) the overmind leaves the body, which has to be supported, either sitting in a chair or lying on a bed or settee. In other words, the infranaut is either fully or semi-unconscious, as in sleep.

With *subjective* clairvoyance, the mind is still conscious and capable of performing various tasks, even complex ones, when and where safe to do so, and, most important, the infranaut can consciously rationalize the experience and observe the action, rather than just becoming a part of it.

The same applies to clairaudience (clear-hearing) and even to psychometry, (tactile clairvoyance) in which impressions are generated in the mind of the person who is handling an object, which can be anything from a letter, or a spectacle case, to a watch or some other personal possession, belonging to another individual.

This was an area of sensitivity in which my father was particularly adept.

Whatever method comes easiest to you is, obviously, the one to use for mental projection, with the equally obvious caveat that these projections should obey the simple rules that my father outlined to me, and that subjective mind-projection should not be practised, while the practitioner is engaged on some task or work, such as driving a car, flying a plane, or operating machinery, that could become dangerous, unless full attention was paid to it.

All this should be self-evident to any sensible person, for in these areas of the mind, *commonsense* is a vitally important asset.

In this chapter, I have dealt mainly with the voluntary opening of the mind, and it follows that, once the mind-channel has been opened, all sorts of unbidden impressions may flood in. So, one of the most important things to remember, at the end of each session of mind projection, is to close the door, which you voluntarily opened when you projected yourself into the realms of the imagination.

This is best done on waking from your experience, by washing your hands in cold water, rinsing from the elbows to the fingers, and wiping away any lingering impressions that you may still retain, especially if they are unpleasant or disturbing. This simple action, in which you pass your hands over your head and flick away the condition that is affecting your aura is both practical and psychological.

'Rubbish!'

You can almost hear the sceptics say the word, with a snort of self-opinionated disgust.

It may seem to be so, at first, but if you think about it, you realize that it is an action which fulfils an effective *psychological* need, by readjusting the mind of the person to the awareness of his or her normal environment, while distancing yourself from any disturbing memories of the experience that the person has just undergone.

If you don't believe that these simple actions are effective, try using them after waking from a bad nightmare, and see how soon you return to normality. Only someone in the most seriously alarmed state fails to respond quickly to these methods.

I know, because I have used these procedures many times, both on myself and on others.

To give you a prime example of how an involuntary OOBE can suddenly manifest to an opened mind, let me tell you an extraordinary experience I underwent in the south of Spain, while writing *The Door Marked Summer*.

I habitually write from the time I wake up, for a period of several hours, because I find that my mind seems to work best first thing in the morning, or, alternatively, late at night. It was a lovely day in Mijas, near Malaga. I was sitting in the garden of the small villa that we were renting, enjoying a cup of coffee and admiring the misty coastline spread out far below me, when suddenly, as clearly as my normal vision, I found myself watching a subjective clairvoyant experience, just like a colour movie, but absolutely silent.

It was so vivid that I gasped, and spilt the coffee.

Before my inner vision passed a series of dramatic images, and from their content it quickly became evident that I was watching an attempt by American Special Forces, to rescue hostages, who, at that time, were being held in Teheran.

This dawned on me soon after the subjective vision started, because I clearly saw a building, several storeys high, with a walled-in compound and a gate, topped with barbed wire, and I, simultaneously, received the impression that this was the United States Embassy in Iran, where the hostages were then being held.

Next I saw a single-decker bus, one of two vehicles which I, somehow, knew had been hijacked by American forces, ram the gate.

At the same time, a number of helicopters appeared, hovering over the compound surrounding the building and American soldiers started to slide down lines, which hung from the machines, as the choppers rapidly approached the ground.

Totally absorbed in the action, my mind abruptly switched to some miles away from this exciting scene and this time I saw big, four-engined Hercules (C.134) transport planes landing at a desert location. At the same time, I received the impression that the helicopters were going to pick up the hostages and fly them out to these transports, for their eventual getaway.

By this time, I was also receiving an equally strong impression that the whole daring operation was going to be a disaster, in direct contrast to the Israeli Raid on the airfield at Entebbe in Africa, which had so successfully released hostages held by terrorists.

This feeling of doom became so horrific, that I switched-off my mind from these alarming visions, and hurried indoors, to tell my wife what I had just experienced, at the same time performing the simple cleansing ritual of washing and wiping away the disturbing residual thoughts.

We both listened to the radio news bulletins, but nothing was said about what I had seen, until it dawned on me that inadvertently I might have been the recipient of a *warning* that this clandestine operation would be a total disaster.

As I had at that time, once again, been brought in contact with security and intelligence forces in Britain, during the dreadful business of investigating our eldest son's death in an accident, I told my wife that I intended to telephone a good friend of mine in Parliament and tell him what I had experienced. This was in the hope that he might be able to warn one of his friends in American Special Forces, perhaps by hinting that he already had received word from abroad that such a raid was being contemplated.

'He will think you've gone potty,' said my wife, with a wry smile.

'I don't think so,' I said. 'His mother was a sensitive and we have discussed these abilities of the mind. He may well listen to what I have to say and warn some American friend, in the American Special Forces. At least it's better than just sitting here, waiting for something dreadful to happen.'

My wise wife had another valid objection to my phoning the House of Commons.

'The local Spanish telephone exchange has an English-speaking operator and there aren't many phones in Mijas. As sure as fate, the operator listens in to any interesting conversations and informs the local Guardia Civil, who will be along to arrest you, as soon as you make that phone call.'

Of course, my wife was right.

Malaga, at that time, was swarming with *contraband-istas* (smugglers) and quite a few foreign Intelligence operatives as well, for this famous Mediterranean port is a sensitive strategic area.

If I had made such a phone call, I probably would have finished up in prison.

Equally obviously, a telegram along similar lines would have brought about the same result.

'I have to do something. I must have picked up that whole operation, perhaps as some kind of warning,' I told Clementina.

She agreed and I quickly composed a letter, putting down the whole experience, and sent it by express mail to my Parliamentary friend, an ex-Special Forces Colonel, at the House of Commons.

About three days later, the disastrous attempt to rescue the hostages took place. The American planes never reached their target, but, instead, suffered a dreadful fatal collision on the ground, in the middle of the desert. Tragically, the whole operation became a shambles, taking the lives of many young American soldiers and airmen.

A few days after this appalling event, I received a letter from my friend in Parliament typed on House of Commons paper.

Dear Michael,

What a rather remarkable coincidence. Your letter arrived on my desk, the morning that the news of the American raid was released. Of course, you didn't get all of it right. For instance, the hijacked buses . . . etc.

The short letter went on, somewhat cautiously, to admit that, in the main, it was an extraordinary occurrence.

A year went by and I related this experience during a lecture which I gave at the Special Forces club. I also mentioned it briefly in one of my books. After the lecture, an American, who was introduced to me as a security expert from the United States Embassy, expressed great interest in my strange story.

He asked me if I would mind one of his colleagues contacting me, when I next visited the States. I agreed to this and the following winter, when I was in California, working on a book, I was telephoned by a member of the Central Intelligence Agency, who asked if he could come down to Palm Springs and interview me.

A couple of days after that, a friendly, extremely tall young American CIA agent identified himself, and, over a curry lunch which I cooked for us, we discussed at length the odd experience that I had undergone in Spain.

'Of course, I didn't get it absolutely right,' I said. 'There was that business about hijacking the buses.'

The CIA man smiled.

'No!' he said. 'You *did* get it right! Part of the plan had been to hijack two local buses and then ram the gates with them, when the helicopters arrived overhead!'

Though he had only been scheduled to visit me for an hour or so, the CIA man stayed with me for seven hours, while we discussed the complex business of the involvement of the paranormal, in clandestine and intelligence operations.

Being a well-trained Intelligence operative, my new friend didn't reveal anything sensitive about United States operations in this special field, but we did talk freely about my own experiences in the Second World War, which I have described fully in my previous books, and the probable use of paranormal methods by the Soviet Union, and other interested countries.

Altogether, it was a fascinating day.

One idea that we both agreed seemed to be valid, was that I had somehow picked-up the thoughts of an American Intelligence officer, closely involved with the whole operation, possibly while he was lying on his bunk, aboard the giant aircraft-carrier from which some of the operation would take off.

The approximate time that I had received the impressions, was around noon Greenwich Mean Time, i.e. in the Gulf area over three hours later in the afternoon when such an unconscious transmission could have been made. At the receiving end was me, a psychic, who, years before, had been trained in Intelligence, and who was relaxing while *writing a book about the paranormal*.

In other words, I was someone who was tuned in to the sort of worried thoughts, that a concerned American Intelligence officer was somehow involuntarily transmitting, as he lay on his bunk in that huge metal aircraft carrier, at sea, somewhere in the approaches to the Arabian Gulf.

When you think about that, it makes good sense, especially as a number of top scientists, such as Professor William Tiller, at the Stanford Research Institute, believe that the key to telepathy and most of the spectrum of paranormal phenomena lies in the extremely low frequency band of electromagnetic transmission and reception.

These are the same frequencies that we use in our minds and we can actually see being automatically scrawled on a continuous chart, recording the electrical activity emanating from the brain of a subject, who is being scanned by an electro-encephalograph attached to his, or her head; the frequencies in question spanning a range of between one cycle per second (1 Hertz) and about 100 Hertz.

So, as you can see, these things are not as crazy as they seem to be on first reading about them.

CHAPTER FIVE

Guides and guidance

One of the earliest concepts of divine guidance was in the form of Angels. In every religion, the Church determines the appropriate dogma and creed and it also formalizes a hierarchy of 'Super Beings'. These archetypes filter the power of divinity down through the ranks of Elohim and Beni Elohim, Archangels, Angels, Princes, *et al.* until the divine power is presumably transformed to a sufficiently low form of energy, which will not blast the human recipient of such angelic force to atoms.

I have no intention of being blasphemous, but that seems to be the basic concept in every religion that I have studied.

From the Old Testament, throughout the New Testament to the Book of Revelations in Christianity in its many forms, in the Torah and the Talmud of the Jewish religion, in the Koran of the Muslims, or the Book of the Dead of the Ancient Egyptians, and even among the Rituals of The Golden Dawn (which were based largely on the *Sacred Magick of Abra-Melin, the Mage*) a divine pecking order is evident.

The same may be said of the mainstream of religious thought throughout the world. In fact, it seems to be one of the cornerstones of religious belief that divine guidance is there for the asking, once the conventions of communication with the Almighty have been established.

I am *not* being irreverent or flippant, but simply stating a fact.

In most contemporary religions, God appears as the Father Figure, the Virgin (Symbol of Purity) as the Mother, and the Son of God becomes the Saviour, in some form.

Allowing for some modification, according to individual dogma and creed, and even taking into account the symbolic animalization of certain divinities, such as in the religion of Ancient Egypt, with its pantheon of attendant gods and goddesses, based on the concept of nature spirits, the pattern of divinity seems to be remarkably similar.

This fact is so marked that many philosophers are of the opinion that *all* these religions appear to have sprung from a common religious root.

Carl Gustav Jung called these 'Super Beings' the 'Archetypes of the Human Collective Unconscious' and went on to describe how they were formed and absorbed into a realm of universal consciousness, which he conceived as surrounding our planet like an aura, and of which we are all a part.

This is the same concept that I came to think of as 'The Universal Over-mind' in parallel with Teilhard de Chardin's *Noosphere* of human intelligence, which the imaginative French priest/scientist believed to be the totality of all human experience, past and present, in the form of an enlightened intellectual atmosphere, co-existent with the ionospheric vault.

The life of this remarkable man spanned the last part of the nineteenth century and continued well into the twentieth, so that his theories can be taken seriously as a valid attempt at the juxtaposition of science and theology. In other words, his spiritual concept of the world was not just the product of dogma and blind faith.

Whatever the belief, the basic concepts of divinity and divine guidance appear to me to have a general similarity, common to all, who believe in the existence of God.

I certainly have no wish to mock any person's subjective beliefs and I respect any creative concept of a power *greater* than that of the individual. I have seen too much of the dreadful results of the alternative belief, in the godless existence of the Superman of the Nazis (based on Nietzche's concept of the Uber-Mensch) or in the appalling regime of Joseph Stalin, to wish to tread that destructive path to chaos. Therefore, I am not an atheist.

I follow my father's advice and always pray for positive guidance, before embarking on any project – such as writing this book – involving my unconscious mind.

This practice of preliminary prayer has become a part of my way of life, especially in anything to do with creative thinking, because I use it as a safeguard, to remind me that my own vanity and arrogance can lead all too quickly to destructive chaos.

From my own experiences, the frightening fact has emerged that the opening of the mind does not, necessarily, run parallel with a seeker's spiritual and moral developement. Obviously, such parallelism is highly desirable for the benefit of all. The alternative can be dangerous, as, for example, with Adolf Hitler, whose mind had been opened to the extent of his possessing remarkable intuition and a vivid imagination, albeit governed by bigotry and melodrama, which served his evil purposes well in the early days of the National Socialist German Workers Party, although in later years he demonstrably lost them, completely.

Therefore I assume that such archetypal guidance as the Führer believed he had received must have originated from the dark side of the universal overmind.

Surely, here is a prime example of the Faustian Pact, leading up to the eventual cashing in of that Demonic agreement which, at some time, Adolf Hitler and his hierarchy had made with their own elastic consciences. It seems to me that this is what the infamous Faustian Pact is all about: a pact made with the lowest side of our nature.

Whether one believes in the existence of the Devil, as an actual living entity, in the terms of Satan and all his legions

93

of Hell, or not, the reality of evil has been demonstrated to the world so often, that no-one can deny its power to destroy all life on earth.

Therefore, such a pact, made with an individual's conscience, whereby any action, no matter how evil and destructive, will be undertaken in order to accomplish some megalomaniacal dream of temporal success, or achievement, can be considered as a Faustian Pact with the embodiment of evil, which is itself a living *force* in the human race.

That is why I do not believe that, in general: 'The ends justify the means'.

For me, this is sufficient reason to pray for positive guidance, before undertaking any task, which could affect the happiness and well-being of others.

God knows, that does not guarantee that such will not be the case, but at least it gives me a yardstick by which to measure the progress of my undertaking, and so far when I listen to that 'still small voice' of my conscience I do not make too many destructive mistakes.

As my father said: 'In this realm of human endeavour, motive is everything.'

I find that caveat to be absolutely valid. Therefore, I accept my own concept of guidance, and find it necessary to say a short prayer for help, before setting out on my journeys into the realms of the collective unconscious, or as I think of it: the universal overmind.

Naturally, this concept of guidance takes on as many forms as there are individuals who seek its aid. However, there are archetypal forms, such as the Holy guardian angels and other spirit guides, which have become common to most religions.

Christians, especially those of the Roman Catholic faith, and the Russian and Greek Orthodoxies, believe in the concept of guidance by Almighty God, through the Blessed Virgin Mary and the Communion of Saints, that hierarchy of risen souls who have attained Sainthood, by being canonized by the leaders of their faith.

94

The religion of Ancient Egypt, with its pantheon of gods and goddesses, who were believed by the priests of Osiris to control the world, can also be seen as the seminal source of Judaeo-Christianity; in the case of the latter religion, having the same concept of a divine Trinity, in the terms of God the Father (Amen-Ra), God the Son (Osiris), and God the Holy Ghost (Horus). Furthermore, the concept of the Blessed Virgin Mary is very similar to that of Isis, the Divine Mother. Again, I have no intention of blaspheming, when pointing out this parallel, for the respective belief in their Divinity is the same.

Having said this, I will try and justify my line of reasoning for the existence of these archetypal figures of cosmos, and their opposing archetypes of chaos.

The Manichaean Heresy, as it was called by the early Roman Catholic church, with which it was co-existent, was practised by the followers of Mane, the Zoroastrian prophet from Persia, who preached the principle of Dualism – the co-existence of Good and Evil.

One could say that what Mane preached can be seen as a parallel, in spiritual terms, to Einstein's theory of the co-existent Dualism of Space and Time, i.e. Space-Time.

The Zoroastrian belief was that good cannot exist, except in terms of evil, neither can evil exist, except in terms of good. Einstein's theory is based on the concept, that Space requires Time during which to occur, just as Time requires Space in which to occur. Therefore, the two entities are totally interdependent; *ergo*, they are one and the same.

Equally, one can argue that positive can only exist in terms of negative, and vice-versa.

The opening mind, for safety's sake, must learn quickly to differentiate between these two opposing forces, even though they are aspects of the same thing, that is, the mental continuum of life.

That is why some form of chart, or symbology, is required, such as that which is embodied in the Cabala, or contained in the teachings of the Tibetan Lamas, or outlined in the Tao, or Zen, to help guide us through the endless labyrinth of inner space.

Surely, this is also what the Ten Commandments are all about.

They are simply practical rules to guide the believer along the straight and narrow path between good and evil, the razor's edge of life.

To the young mind which is being trained for these voyages into the imagination, this guidance is all-important. For me, my father was my guide, because I trusted him completely and loved him very much, therefore, he represented for me the archetype of a spirit guide.

Let us pause for a moment to define what is meant by an archetype.

In the dictionary, the word archetype is defined as: 'The original model or pattern, on which future copies are based.'

For instance, if I say to you: 'Sherlock Holmes', you immediately visualize a tall, gaunt man, with acquiline features, clothed in a Norfolk jacket, or a caped Inverness overcoat, wearing a deerstalker hat, smoking a calabash-shaped pipe and possibly holding a large magnifying glass.

This is the archetype of the 'Great Detective'.

If, on the other hand, I say: 'Robin Hood', you probably visualize an archer, brawny and bearded, with a face tanned by living rough in Sherwood Forest, and dressed in Lincoln Green, to blend in with the forest. This is the archetype of the outlaw, who robs the rich to give to the poor as the symbol of rebellion against tyranny.

The chances are that both these archetypal images will be vividly depicted in your imagination. Yet, *neither of them ever existed*, except in the minds of the authors who created them.

In all fairness, there is some speculation that Robin Hood was the nickname given to a freeman, one Robin Locksley, who later is believed to have become the Earl of

Huntingdon when King Richard the Lion Heart returned from the Third Crusade. Also, for a time, he was supposed to have been outlawed by King John, but this story is based on the slimmest of evidence taken from ballads and medieval literature.

The author who finally brought this ancient legend to literary life was Sir Walter Scott, who gave his hero, Ivanhoe, a staunch ally in Robin Locksley, the leader of the outlaws in Sherwood Forest. Scott was working mainly from legend, when he created his masterpiece, *Ivanhoe*, and he drew heavily on this archetypal myth.

As we all know, Sherlock Holmes was the wonderful creation of another great storyteller, Sir Arthur Conan Doyle. Apparently, he based his master-detective on the composite characters of two of his friends, one of whom, like himself, was a doctor.

In both cases, these archetypal figures have settled deeply into the collective unconscious, and can be recalled instantly by those familiar with their legends. There is a bronze statue of Robin Hood in Sherwood Forest and many visitors from around the world, especially from the United States, come to London, often specifically, to seek out 'Number 221b, Baker Street', a house that has never existed, but which was created by Conan Doyle, as the residence of Sherlock Holmes and Doctor Watson.

That is how vividly these archetypes of the universal overmind can become part of our race-memory.

This then probably is the source from which you will visualize your guide, to help you find your way through the endless maze of the imagination.

Our powers of creating mental images, no matter how they manifest to our unconscious minds, are only bound by the extent of our knowledge, or our acquaintance with everything that we have previously experienced. Nevertheless, I also believe that we are all influenced by other experiences, inherited by us from our ancestors, through the race-memory of our species.

Does this race-memory really exist?

There are a number of different opinions about it. My argument is that if the mitocondriae, those millions of microscopic chemical factories which control the genetic system of our bodies, determine how every individual cell will recreate itself, in its own image, during the on-going, seven-year physical regeneration cycle, then the dominant genes in the body could also transmit the inherited race-memory to each new generation.

In the case of brain cells, these do *not* regenerate during the seven-year cycle, but grow until we are adult. We have trillions of them, so that our brain-power lasts us throughout most of our normal lifespan of some seventy years.

The problem is: how can one argue a case for the inheritance of such a race-memory?

If you look at photographs, or portraits of your ancestors, whose likenesses were recorded in some accurate fashion, you may be surprised by the close resemblance between yourself and those of your forebears who evidently passed down their dominant genes to you.

Therefore, if the chemistry of the mitocondriae in our bodies can determine the shape of our features, our general build, the shape and form of our hands and feet, our probable length of lifespan, our colouring, height and many other factors, which, evidently, have been passed down to us by heredity; why then should not the dominant memory-patterns of these same ancestors also be passed on to posterity?

How often have you heard: 'You are just like your mother . . . or father, or grandfather, grandmother, or some other distant relative.'? Then photographs or portraits have been produced, to back up the statement.

I certainly have had this experience on a number of occasions.

Furthermore, I also have heard:'You are so like your grandfather *in character* . . . or this or that great-uncle or great-aunt', none of whom I ever had known. Yet the resemblance, in either appearance or character, was noticed by some elderly relative, who had known them, in childhood.

This might even prove to be another explanation of the phenomenon of 'déjà-vu', that strange feeling people occasionally experience of having been somewhere before, when, in fact, it is the first time that they have actually visited the place.

One popular explanation is that, for a moment, on entering the room, the mind may have blanked out for an instant, and when it regained its normal function, the impression given was that the person had seen the room before, which, of course, is what he or she *had* just done.

But supposing that an ancestor, not necessarily a distant one, whose dominant genes you had inherited, had been a previous visitor to this place and it was his or her memory-pattern that had given you the impression that you had been there before?

That might well explain your own sense of having been there, as well as the feeling that you know exactly what is round the corner in the next room.

At least it is an interesting thought.

Spiritualists believe that they have spirit guides, who help them during the crises in their lives. Often, these guides are described as being North American Indians, Chinese sages, Atlantean High-priests, Incas, Indian Gurus, Tibetan Lamas and other exotic beings, all of whom, presumably, qualify for the role of guide, by reason of their having lived close to Nature, or being spiritually enlightened in some other way. At least, that is how it has been explained to me, by reasonable and rational friends, who firmly believe in such beings.

I am *not* scoffing at Spiritualists for their beliefs, for I have shared many of their paranormal experiences, but, as a seeker after truth I try to be as open-minded as possible and, therefore, I tend not to *join* any particular religious group nor do I wish to be flippant about anyone else's strongly-held, subjective beliefs.

However, it always has seemed strange to me that few spirit guides purport to be the discarnate souls of ordinary folk, with a less romantic background, like that of a district nurse, a gardener, a fisherman, or a farmer, all of whom often live equally close to Nature, and can be very enlightened, yet who seldom, if ever, seem to get a look-in as a spirit guide.

My late daughters, Marylla and Elaine, both believed that they had lived previous lives, and that they were suffering in this life (they both died of cancer) to fulfil some aspect of their Karma, the path of spiritual enlightenment gained by experience that eventually leads towards perfection – but only after the experience of many life-times.

I certainly would not argue with the theory of Reincarnation, because the concept of Karma seems to be such a logical one, as a form of spiritual progression, having much in common with Darwin's theory of Evolution.

But I do have certain objections, such as, when at present there are over five billion souls incarnate on this earth, how could those same entities have all lived during historical eras, when say only six hundred million people, or less, were living on our planet.

Reincarnationists tend to visualize their past lives in terms of the Ancient Egyptians, early Greek or Roman dignitaries, slave-girls or gladiators, Napoleonic soldiers, French revolutionaries or aristocrats, and other romantic figures of the historical past. Frankly, I don't see how so many souls could all fit into the comparatively few bodies available at those specific times.

The usual answer to this rational objection is that we live, and have lived, in a multi-dimensional continuum, with many parallel planes of simultaneous existence, which, I freely admit, is an argument that fits in well with Einstein's theories and contemporary scientific thought, which is centred round the probability of the existence of such parallel continuums, but which is also extremely difficult to conceive, other than in mathematical, i.e. symbolic terms.

Yet, essentially, this is also the continuum of the imagination.

Consequently, I am not going to ridicule anyone's concept of reincarnation, least of all those beliefs held by my late, dearly-loved elder daughters.

It is evident to me that, in the boundless and near-inconceivable realms of creative imagination, seekers badly need a guide, to show them the way and bring them safely back into their bodies, during their periods of transcendental meditation, or other OOBEs.

Otherwise, as I have already pointed out a number of times, there is considerable psychological danger involved. Consequently, it seems to me that guides may well be drawn from among the archetypes of the collective unconscious, or universal overmind, as the need arises.

The choice of a particular archetype may depend on the unconscious desire of the person who seeks guidance, and often the preference may be for a mentor who has lived close to Nature and therefore, presumably, has a greater appreciation of the intangible side of life, rather than its material aspect.

Under the spiritual law of 'like attracts like', in terms of character and aesthetic awareness, the archetype best suited to the seeker's mentality would manifest as the spirit guide, or even as the Holy guardian angel.

This does not seem to be illogical, as a method by which spirit guides, in the spiritualist sense, are drawn towards certain people with specific needs. This could also explain why healers, with genuine ability to transfer their own over-abundant energies to other, less fortunate people, often believe they have spirit guides, who, during their earth-life, had been doctors or surgeons.

This was the sort of claim made by that remarkable psychic, Edgar Cayce, who confounded a number of members of the twentieth-century medical profession by his apparently extensive knowledge of medicine, even though he had received no formal training whatsoever in that art. According to a number of highly-qualified observers, among whom were physicians and surgeons, Cayce had an exceptional gift of accurate diagnosis, which he ascribed to the medical knowledge and past experience of his spirit guides.

As I neither knew nor worked with Edgar Cayce, I can only give this information from hearsay, or books, but, if my theory is correct, this medium was probably in contact with archetypes of the collective unconscious who were associated with the art of medicine. Alternatively, a spiritualist would believe that Cayce was being controlled by a discarnate entity, who had been a doctor on earth, and I don't intend to reject that concept, either.

But, to me, what matters is successful healing, rather than the specific method by which it is accomplished, because, in all his cases, this remarkable American medium seems to have given some extraordinarily accurate diagnoses and, furthermore, to have prescribed the most beneficial treatments, which, apparently, cured his patients.

No skilled physician could have done more.

However, I have seen and recorded some remarkable cases of healing in my previous books, and I am convinced that whollistic healing can work – in many cases dramatically well.

Sadly, it is always difficult to find a genuine healer, and, at present, the mainstream of psychic healing also includes many self-deluded practitioners, and even, regrettably, quite a few downright charlatans, who unforgivably batten on to the suffering of others.

If healing is not considered to be an alternative to the art of conventional medicine, but rather is accepted as a *complementary* adjunct to it, I feel that it can be beneficial – even if the benefit is in the patient's improved morale and therefore mainly psychological.

Either way it is beneficial!

It is only when a charlatan, or a self-deluded healer, takes preference over conventional medical care, to the exclusion of the skills of qualified doctors and surgeons, that the danger becomes apparent.

Having said that, in all fairness, I must point out that I know of several authenticated cases, where conventional medicine has failed and a patient, usually in a terminal condition, has turned to a genuine healer and thereby received great benefit, even in cases of terminal cancer, when total remission was experienced following the healing.

In the cases of both my late daughters, I saw the benefit to their general morale and peace of mind, which genuine healing brought to them.

Tragically, it was too late to effect a cure, or a remission, in view of the extent of their previous radical surgery, but it was certainly most effective in helping them to bear the suffering of terminal cancer, which conventional medicine could only treat with morphine, pethedine and the use of other dangerous drugs and pain-killers.

During these sad times, I have spoken to a number of specialists, who confirmed my impression that the cancer patient's psychological condition can directly affect the rate of growth of malignant tumours.

For instance, at the Royal Marsden Hospital, two doctors told me that if a patient has domestic problems, the rate of deterioration in their condition and the growth of malignant tumours increased rapidly. Conversely, if these personal problems were solved and the patient's morale was restored, there often was a significant improvement in their condition, or even a remission, in the course of the disease.

I was present, with my wife, when both my elder daughters died, one of them in my arms, and I have no doubt that I sensed the exact moment when the spirit, or if you prefer it the personality, left their bodies.

Naturally, the feeling of grief was overwhelming, but my subjective beliefs have helped me to ease that pain and to accept their deaths, as a stage in their continuity as a part of the universal overmind.

I wish others could learn to bear the same agonizing pain and ease it in a similar way. I can assure my readers that I saw the look of joy and relief on both my daughters' faces, whenever their healers arrived. I can never repay the kindness of Doris Collins and especially Betty Shine for all their healing efforts. God bless them both! In fact, it is something that I will never forget, and neither will my wife.

I know that I could not have continued to work in comedy, after the deaths of three of my splendid children, had I not been trained to open my mind, by my father and mother. Furthermore, in the case of our eldest son, Stuart, who died in a mysterious light-aircraft crash which I then had to investigate, that nightmare was only resolved by my wartime training in Intelligence, combined with my open-minded attitude to the tragedy and its frightening aftermath.

At the time I was very aware of being in receipt of guidance, and I sensed very strongly that this mentor was my father. Had I not carried out what I believe to have been my father's explicit instructions, during that horrific two-year period, I would never have come out of it, with my sanity still intact.

You may have noted that I do not mention my mother, as often as I do my father. This has nothing to do with lack of love for Ma, who had a very strong influence on my life, especially in developing my sense of humour, and I also owe her an enormous debt of gratitude for her practical commonsense, wisdom, and love, which she gave to both my brother and myself. But it was, principally, my father, who helped me to develop my awareness of the vastness and power of the infinite realms of the imagination, and who safely opened my mind for me.

Therefore, as this book is about that subject, I tend to mention Pop rather more than I do Ma.

Incidentally, my father believed he had two spirit guides, for although he was not a spiritualist, he agreed with some of their beliefs.

These guides were both fascinating examples of archetypes of the collective unconscious. I will try to describe them, as accurately as I can recall.

When they manifested through my father, they were quite different. One of them, whom I came to think of as: 'The little old man', when he was in control, actually seemed to shrink my father's already compact body, and manifested so strongly that he actually appeared to *age* Pop, covering his face with a network of fine lines, such as one would expect to see in the features of an octogenarian.

This guide claimed to have been a monkish philosopher from the seventeenth century, and, during many sessions with my father, sitting in full light, in a trance, he imparted some remarkable knowledge, in reply to my searching questions, all of which information was later proven to be 100 per cent correct. This included details of events in the forthcoming war, my future career and even totally accurate predictions regarding future space flight

That, in itself, is remarkable.

The other guide was a Chinese doctor, who manifested quite differently, by seeming to fill out my father's face, so that it became plumper, bland and almost *unlined*; the eyes, in particular, taking on the appearance of an Oriental person. Again, to be scrupulously fair, Pop, being Peruvian by origin, had certain inherited racial characteristics in his features, due to his line of descent being part-Spanish, from the time of the Conquistadors, and part-Inca, from my ancestors' intermarriage with the people they had conquered.

Therefore, it was not too difficult for a Chinese physiognomy to appear on my father's features although I must point out that Pop's face, when under the control of this guide, became unmistakably Oriental and was quite different from his usual appearance.

105

Furthermore, the two contrasting voices, which seemed to speak through my father, were very distinctive and totally different. Even allowing for the fact that an individual voice-print, no matter how you disguise it, is as distinctive as a fingerprint, I vividly recall two completely *different* voices manifesting, in turn, as each guide spoke through my father.

Once again, in the interests of truth, I would like to point out that Pop was a keen amateur actor, of considerable ability, which is probably why I inherited a certain facility as a character-comedian. My brother and I were both brought up with an awareness of our parents' talents. That is why I am absolutely *certain* that, in neither case, were these two distinctive guides merely projections of my father's ability as an amateur actor, because they were outside his usual range of characterization. I have several other reasons for believing that these two spirit guides were genuine examples of their genre.

First, why should my father seek to fool a thirteen-year-old boy, when he himself was such a stickler for truth in his researches? That just doesn't make sense.

Second, I already was familiar with my father's different characters, which he played in various local amateur theatrical productions. None of them remotely fitted the personality of either of these two guides.

Third, I cannot see how the extraordinary accuracy of the predictive information, which was given me by both of them, could have been known to my father, as some of it only became demonstrably accurate many years later.

Consequently, although I would not offer this as conclusive proof of the existence of spirit guides, it remains for me part of an intriguing puzzle.

The guide who attached himself to our family circle, back in the thirties, and manifested unmistakably through the sessions with the rocking table, gave his name as Tom Shepherd. His characteristic presence was indicated by the table being rocked five times, followed by the distinctive way in which his messages were spelled out. As

106

I have explained, the different styles of operating this table-turning, gave an immediate indication of the change of operator, as with all Morse-code transmissions.

Tom Shepherd purported to be the soul of an eighteenth-century doctor, and acted as the 'doorkeeper' to our home-circle. He explained that so many entities were eager to manifest through the channel of the table, in order to give evidence of their survival and send loving messages to their families, that it was necessary to regulate the traffic. (My word not his.)

This conjured up the picture of an 'Other World' telephone box, with a long queue of eager souls impatiently waiting their turn, but, in a strange way, it also made sense. Later, during the war, I often saw the earthly equivalent of this spiritual queue, with eager aircrew standing in a frustrated line outside a single telephone box in the village near the airfield, trying to get through to their families to reassure them that they were alive and well after their previous night's air raid on Germany.

When you imagine the same scene, translated into the terms of our home-circle, and a similar number of desperate souls, on the 'Other Side', all with the same compulsive motive of wishing to reassure their families of their survival, Tom Shepherd's strange statement that he acted as the 'doorkeeper' makes sense.

I am aware of the experiments in Toronto, carried out by a group of young psychologists, using the same method of table-turning, with the object of synthesizing the sort of entities, who manifest through this unusual method of communication. The experiments succeeded in projecting a synthetic entity, whom the researchers called Phillip and to whom they gave certain characteristics, which, previously, had been agreed between them. After the group had concentrated for a number of sessions on the creation of this non-existent person, Phillip manifested through the table and manipulated it in the usual fashion.

I believe that the team of researchers created an archetype of the collective unconscious, as real, in their minds, as Sherlock Holmes or Robin Hood. I also believe that they could have done exactly the same thing with those two famous literary archetypes, had they gone about the experiment in the same way, but using them as the syntheses.

What matters in the early stages of opening the mind, is that all these mental exercises should proceed in an orderly and reasoned manner, at properly determined intervals, and without any danger of overtiring the experimenters. Nor should any part of these exercises ever be allowed to become obsessive.

I cannot overemphasize that proviso, because I have seen a number of people go about this type of research in the *wrong* way and finish up, at best, with a nervous breakdown.

In Rudyard Kipling's words: 'I have seen too much evil and sorrow and wreck of good minds on the road to Endor to take one step along that perilous track.'

These are the words of a frightened man, which is something that, normally, that great writer was not. Yet this same remarkable man gives total credit for his ability to write to his personal 'daemon', as he refers to his Muse:

This is the doom of the Makers – Their daemon lives in their pen
If he be absent or sleeping, they are even as other men.
But if he be utterly present, and they swerve not from his behest,
The word that he gives shall continue, whether in earnest or jest.

To avoid being accused of sexism, I should point out that this stanza applies equally to women authors, and I believe that Daphne du Maurier sensed a similar inspirational presence when writing her splendidly imaginative romances. Furthermore, my friend, Brian Inglis, in his fascinating book, *The Unknown Guest*, also touches on this phenomenon of apparent inspirational guidance, quoting, among others, Kipling, and Graham Greene.

Such guidance to me is as real as the sun rising each dawn, and I have learnt from experience that, if I am not being guided, I might just as well stop trying to create anything.

Furthermore, I have noticed that I usually have to ask for this assistance, in the form of a short silent prayer, and I know that it will not be granted to me, until I have done everything in my power to advance the work, myself.

Among the many show-business personalities whom I know well, a number of them frequently consult mediums, at difficult times in their professional or personal lives, and one of them, an extremely nice and talented person, whom I will not embarrass by naming, recently had some very remarkable evidence given him regarding his future career, indicating a totally unexpected success, of such proportions that it would radically alter his whole life.

He had telephoned and asked to come and see me on the spur of the moment, even though he only knew me slightly, because he had become somewhat concerned about his professional life. This is by no means unusual among artists, as their art, by its ephemeral nature, is mercurial in character, and tends to lead them into periods of despondency, when things don't seem to be going well. Such is the nature of our unstable and demanding profession.

During the course of our conversation, I was strongly impressed by the sincerity and integrity of this actor, whom I had long admired both as a person and as a professional and I was delighted to pick-up a strong impression that a new show was in the pipeline for him, and furthermore that it would be a resounding success.

I told him so and he grinned: 'I sure hope you're right, Mike.'

He then asked me if I knew a good medium whom he might consult and I gave him the name of a close friend of mine, who I felt would be the ideal person for him to consult.

I phoned her to check that she was available and told her that she could expect a phone call from an actor friend of mine. Apart from that, as is my custom, I passed no other information to her, as this would only lessen the impact of any evidence that she might give to her prospective client. I was delighted when my actor friend phoned me, some days later, to tell me that the medium, Betty Shine, had confirmed my 'impression' of an impending show for which he was, unknowingly, being considered.

Furthermore, she had given him some extraordinary evidence concerning his past life, which was not public knowledge, and had predicted a glowing future for his career, which at that time he had believed to be in the doldrums.

He was so obviously delighted by the results of his consultation that he frequently telephoned the medium and received further guidance.

Her predictions of his future outstanding success were borne out 100 per cent and I am happy to say that today he is in a powerful position in our profession.

When my late daughter, 'Fusty' (Marylla), was dying, he very kindly sent her a gift of his latest recording, which had not yet been released to the public. As I mentioned, he is an extremely nice person, and we are all delighted that he has done so well, for he is now in a strong position to help others, which I am sure he will take every opportunity of doing.

I can well understand why he does not wish to make this information public, in view of the way that the Press, undoubtedly, would treat him. But if he ever wishes to do so, I am sure that this would help many other people, who are as much in need of guidance as he was when, in a moment of anxiety, he rang me.

Although my own family have suffered tragic personal losses and been through a number of very bad times, even experiencing what the chief Exorcist of the Church of

110

England described as a psychic attack, I know that there is nothing to fear, so long as I keep faith with my guides, in whom I have complete confidence.

Furthermore, I believe that, under the natural *law* of 'like attracts like', these guides are my personal *intuitive* selection from the archetypes of the human unconscious.

I also feel that, without them and their positive guidance, I would soon become hopelessly lost in the boundless universe of the imagination.

CHAPTER SIX

Please leave this place in the state in which you would wish to find it

This earth that we treat so carelessly is not only our place of residence, we also are made of it.

We ignore this fact at our peril!

As the, supposedly, most intelligent species on the earth, when it comes to our behaviour, we act like hooligans, destroying and defacing both the ecology and the ethology of the planet, of which we are an integral part. The plain fact is that we are not acting sanely.

Even when we depict Nature, on film or television, the programmes so often dwell, lovingly, on animals tearing each other apart or insects gobbling up their prey. How often have I viewed this sort of grisly scene and switched off. Yet the self-appointed pundits, who are supposed to monitor this kind of gratuitous violence, tolerate it without question, because it is classed as educational, and therefore, presumably, directed mainly at young audiences.

Violence and death are part of Nature, in its cycle of survival, but why must they be emphasized with such glee?

It all seems to stem from our enjoyment of violence, as a form of entertainment. You can even buy or rent videotapes with titles like 'Great Disasters of the World.'

Our television and cinema screens are filled with top-earning horror movies, such as the mindless sadism of *Nightmare on Elm Street*, with its anti-hero, 'Freddie', a particularly nasty example of special-effects make-up and ingenious trick photography, that sends children to bed, shivering with terror, or, even worse, conditions their young minds to accept this sort of ghoulish horror as a normal part of life.

When I was a boy, *Frankenstein* and *Dracula* were examples of the horror genre of movie-making and were relatively mild, their violence being largely implicit, and imagined off-screen, in stark contrast to today's ghastly visual presentations in full colour and explicit detail; yet, they were still frightening enough to scare the wits out of many youngsters, including me.

From the twenties, right up to the abolition of strict screen censorship in the mid-sixties, all films, in this country and the USA, were made under the rigid censorship and control of the Hays Office, in America, and the British Board of Film Censors, in the United Kingdom.

Today, only token lip-service is being paid to grading these explicitly horrific movie and video presentations, by tagging them with such labels as Adult, X-rated, Parental guidance required, Not suitable for young children, unless accompanied by an adult, etc., for projection in cinemas, or not to be shown before 9 o'clock at night and other feeble labels.

These procedures do little or nothing to stop them being viewed by an enormous number of children, who seem to have little parental control over their TV and video viewing.

This sort of on-screen violence, backed up by the frightening increase in the sale of horror comics, in which every nasty sado-masochistic perversion of the human mind is reproduced, with a drooling fidelity to detail, is bound to have a deleterious effect on young minds and may lead to the growth of savage teenage and adult crime on a frightening scale.

Most of these crimes of extreme violence, resulting in severe injuries and often death, are being carried out with weapons, like those popularized by the Ninja films and videos, and even with illegally obtained guns, which were seldom, if ever before, used by such young delinquents.

Talking to headmasters and the staffs of schools, in both Britain and the United States, is alarming, when you find the same sense of despair manifested in their stories of extreme playground violence, inspired by the constant presentation of perverted martial arts on the small screen.

Even responsible news programmes seem particularly pleased with themselves, when they show extremely violent scenes of battle, revolution, disaster, or dreadful accidents of any kind, in gory detail, at any hour of the day or night, usually without warning the viewers of the horrors to come.

Television producers of these programmes have told me: 'It significantly increases the viewing figures.'

Then, if people complain, they are either fobbed-off with excuses, or find themselves open to accusations of having Fascist tendencies by promoting censorship, and thereby interfering with the sacred 'Freedom of the Press'.

Freedom of expression is a most valuable part of our precious democratic heritage and should be preserved as a symbol of our hard-won liberty, but it should never be used as a front by those whose sole purpose for being in the media is to make as big a profit as they can, commercially or politically, no matter what the content of their programmes may be.

Liberty is one thing. *Licence* is something quite different!

What applies to the written word, in responsibly edited newspapers, magazines and periodicals, or the spoken word, on radio, where freely-stated and considered opinions should have the democratic right to be read and heard, can hardly apply to many of the presentations on the hypnotic, and addictive, medium of television.

Nowadays, TV is in most people's homes, with a rapidly growing proportion of viewers in most Third

World countries. Young children everywhere can have easy access to explicit horror, in both factual and fictional programmes. This unacceptable state of affairs has resulted, to date, in a terrifying rise in the growth-rate of violent crime, especially among juveniles, with some of these tragedies being the result of sexual perversions of the worst kind.

It cannot be just coincidence that, in every democratic country, where the Ideal of freedom from Press censorship is quite rightly upheld, this dramatic rise in violent crime is demonstrably parallel to the growth of explicit violence in television. It is rapidly becoming a global problem, with the introduction of satellite-relayed TV transmissions.

Radio, alone, even when backed by a graphically pictorial press, could never have had this effect, unless it had been deliberately angled, as it was under the Nazi regime, who used broadcasting as a weapon.

After forty-two years in the media I am convinced that television, more than all other forms of the media, can be held responsible for the under-controlled visual presentation of violence, inside the homes of the viewing public, and that is, in the descriptive words of Karl Marx: 'A crime against the People'.

What is all this leading up to?

I am as deeply concerned about the *mental* pollution of the ethology of our country, as I am about the widespread harm that has been inflicted on the *physical* ecology of Britain and much of the rest of the world, by those who are solely motivated by profit, or by other compulsive motives, such as the acquisition of power for its own sake.

Hence the title of this chapter: 'Please leave this place in the state in which you would wish to find it.'

I can almost hear the cries of: 'When does the book-burning begin?'

Let us all hope: Never!

But that does not mean that all reasonable guidelines of commonsense must also be rejected. Far from it!

Too often, the hysterical and extremist viewpoint of fanatical do-gooders becomes the battlecry of those in positions of media power, who cynically manipulate this small, but vociferous section of public opinion, for their own purposes, often drowning out the sensible voices of reason, which are also being raised against these manipulators' *own* excesses.

Their slogan seems to be: 'Don't do what I do. Do what I tell you!'

Once again, and I cannot stress this point too strongly, it is simply a question of commonsense, i.e. the reasonable consideration of each case, on its own merits and disadvantages.

These same extremists, who so loudly advocated the rights of a permissive society, have also been at least partly instrumental in the rise, among other horrors, of incurable AIDS, with its resultant life-threatening situation, where blood-banks are being contaminated by the deadly virus. They must also take some responsibility for the dramatic increase in venereal diseases, due to wholesale promiscuity and widespread drug addiction, especially among the young.

Such extremism has often brought discredit to the reasonable, sane arguments of the true liberals, whose conscience and commonsense can be an effective brake against excessive militancy, on the part of both the extreme right and the extreme left political wings.

That is why the normal democratic process is so slow. Because it takes time to make up its mind. That is what the ideal of democracy should be about: government by the will of the people, after proper thought and discussion has been given to their problems.

However, where the media is largely, or completely, under the control of powerful pressure-groups, with little or no conscience to guide them, there is grave danger to the ethology of that country.

All of which is why I believe in the maxim: 'Eternal Vigilance is the Price of Liberty.'

That is also why I am convinced that the only way we can live as free men and women, within the parameters of self-disciplined consideration for our fellow-passengers on this earth, is to open our minds and try to understand the sort of pressures to which, consciously or unconsciously, we are constantly being subjected.

How can we recognize these subtle attacks on our invaluable ethology of liberty, which we should prize as highly as we do our health and the pursuit of happiness, because it is the product of so many people's lives, over thousands of years of toil, suffering and sacrifice?

We can do this by using our open-minded intuition, filtered by commonsense, and carefully evaluating all the statements being made to us, by those who are trying to manipulate our minds, for political and commercial purposes.

One of the techniques which I have learned to use, as a direct route to my unconscious mind, and, at times, to the collective unconscious, or universal overmind, (as I think of it) is that of dowsing, or divining. Those two words only refer to the same ability of a person, or an animal, to contact the instinctive side of the mind.

Ideally, this contact should be unclouded by wishful thinking, and this is one of the difficulties that the practitioners of these techniques have to overcome. Naturally, as in all forms of decision-making, this is not easy to do.

One of the mandatory thought-processes that must be used in this situation, is to weigh carefully the degree of wishful thinking that is likely to be present in each question and answer; for that is the basic form in which dowsing, or divining should be employed if it is to be effective.

So far, all this is fairly obvious.

Let us now proceed with caution.

As a boy, I first became attracted to these techniques, when I witnessed a skilled water-diviner, as he was then called, in action successfully locating an abundant source of pure water on farmland in Kent.

When I asked my father about this water-witch, as they were known locally, and how much of his skill could be put down to pure luck, he told me that his ability was an ancient art, and, as such, was difficult to turn on and off, at will.

'This is why it is always so tricky to test mediums, diviners and other sensitives, in terms of empiric, repeatable experiments, because a living being does not respond to the same tests, in an identical way, at different times,' my father told me. 'We are continually changing, fractionally, minute by minute, due to the natural process of cellular regeneration, and the daily loss of part of our brain-cells, which, after we become adult, degenerate and do not, like our body cells, renew themselves. Moreover, chemically speaking, we also change quite significantly every time we eat, or drink, digest, urinate or defecate.

'Therefore, a series of empiric experiments, even under ideal laboratory conditions, and carried out with exactly the same procedures on a living subject, will seldom come up with similar results. Furthermore, the researchers themselves are constantly changing, as well.'

My father continued, as nearly as I can remember his words: 'The implications become clear when the scientist is conducting experiments, using sensitives as the subject of research. Due to their sensitivity as artists, because that is what they are, these subjects tend to become tense, under clinical test conditions and often will negate their own performance, in whatever sphere of the paranormal they are being evaluated.

'This is much the same situation that faces actors at auditions, or confronts artists, who are having to show their abilities to those who have no understanding of art, and I am told that a feeling of having butterflies

118

in the stomach is experienced by anyone, who is being interviewed for the first time on radio (which was the most nerve-wracking medium of that period).

'It is because of this, that so few genuine sensitives show up well, when being given scientific tests by methods which originally were developed to evaluate the properties of minerals, chemical elements, gases and other inorganic substances.

'What we need is a new set of guidelines, based on our ability to test sensitives, while they are performing their particular branch of the arts. So far, Michael, we have not come up with these tests, nor have we built any instruments, sensitive enough to tell us what a person is thinking, or even whether that thought is creative or destructive.'

That in essence and as near as I can remember it, is what my father told me and the more I think about them, the more valid his words become.

The main instruments that scientists possessed in the late thirties, were the early electro-encephalographs and electro-cardiograms which could detect electrical emissions from the brain and the pattern of heartbeats, respectively, plus Gauss meters and crude magnetometers, to measure the strength of an electric field. Besides this equipment, they had copper-mesh Faraday cages, to exclude outside electrical interference, and used thermometers and sphygnomanometers for taking body temperature and blood-pressure.

Apart from these few instruments of limited sensitivity, we had no instruments capable of accurately quantifying or qualifying human, or even animal, thought processes.

Even today, we still have no such instruments, though we are now attempting to construct cybernetic (robot) machines capable of limited artificial intelligence.

Therefore, it follows that our bodies and brains are infinitely more complex and capable of a far greater range of thought-processes, than any of the machines or instruments which we invent, in order to increase the speed of our mathematical calculations and our faculties of sight, hearing, taste, touch and smell.

We use machines to help us to multiply our strength in mechanical handling, and these combined with sophisticated instrumentation are capable of safely transporting us by land, sea and air. They have helped us to reach the moon, and our space-probes reach the outer planets of our solar system.

One day, they may take us to the stars; that is if we don't succeed in destroying ourselves first by the misapplication of our own ingenuity.

Once more, I return to the hypothesis, which I learned from my father and which I only accepted, after he had proved it to me, beyond reasonable doubt.

'Imagination is more important than knowledge.'

The same words that, years later, I read, when I was studying, with difficulty, the works of Professor Albert Einstein. In that great man's words: 'Imagination is more important than knowledge, because each *new* idea increases the sum total of knowledge, by that one new thought.'

It was only after working with my friends, Colin Bloy and his brother David, who are both exceptional dowsers, that I realized that dowsing is a basic, inherent ability in animals and humans, by which, among other things, the presence of underground water can be detected by the use of intuition, coupled directly with the normal thought-processes of the conscious mind.

This demonstrable ability to find subterranean water is only the take-off point for the many other applications of the dowser's art: for that is what it is, an art, and like all artists, dowsers are better at one or other application of their abilities, and vary in the effectiveness of their performance, at different times.

Here are just some of the many other uses for the practice of dowsing.

(1) Detecting the presence and extent of mineral deposits, such as gold, silver and oil, etc.

(2) Finding the course of subterranean electricity cables, and gas-pipes.

(3) Charting the outline of underground chambers and buried buildings.

(4) Using dowsing to back-up conventional medical diagnostic skill.

(5) Finding missing objects.

(6) Locating missing persons, alive or dead, by dowsing charts.

(7) Detecting lines and fields of force, not necessarily apparent to contemporary instrumentation, and many other uses, besides.

All of which sounds pretty far-fetched.

That is what I thought until, after a ten-year period of detailed research and demonstrations by many dowsers, of both sexes and all ages, with whom I also had long discussions, and much personal experimentation, I became convinced that dowsing is a valid art and is far more commonly used than I had ever imagined.

Is this art such a strange manifestation of the abilities of our minds?

Who would have thought that Michelangelo Buonarroti could have seen his finished masterpiece of the *Pieta*, in the section of rock-face that he chose to be cut out of the marble quarry wall?

Who believed Nikola Tesla, when he first described his clearly-imagined ideas for the epoch-making alternating-current induction motor, which gave the world a practical system of electrical power and led us into the twentieth century?

Who, before the First World War, could have conceived that the key to the terrifying power of nuclear energy, and the potential destruction of all life on earth, lay in the complex equations of Albert Einstein, then an obscure patent clerk in Zurich?

How many people recognized the young carpenter from Nazareth, for what He really was, and what His teachings would do to the world?

I can make out a long list of gifted men and women, who suffered the jibes and scorn of the omniscient Establishment and its sycophants, even after the true value of their great work became evident to those with open minds.

The Impressionists, like Monet, Manet, Cézanne, Sisley, Gauguin, and Van Gogh, whose paintings were jeered at and mocked when they were first exhibited, are only one collective example of this sort of persecution.

It isn't only today that we suffer from the opinions of the instant expert, fresh from a college degree. Every era in history has had similar pundits, who, unasked, gave the world: 'The benefit of their ignorance'. They seldom, if ever, make a close and detailed examination of the subject of their scorn, preferring to damn it out of hand, if that is the way that the popular current of public opinion flows.

But, conversely, these same, self-appointed judges of our abilities suddenly fall silent, once a new and original accomplishment, which they have loudly derided, is eventually accepted and absorbed by the scientific or artistic hierarchy of the Establishment, who also never apologize to those whom they have persecuted. Instead, these self-appointed inquisitors become instant experts on the subject, which they so recently condemned.

Sadly, this seems to be a part of human nature.

I did not accept dowsing as a fact of life, until I had witnessed numerous valid demonstrations over a ten-year period, and had personally developed this ability to a sufficient degree to check the results for myself. But I certainly didn't deride the dowsers and their efforts during that long investigation!

The experiments we conducted together, and the things that I subsequently found out for myself, opened for me another vast realm of the imagination. That is what dowsing is all about: using the circuitry of the body and the sensitivity of the mind, through the imagination, to detect the presence, or absence, of whatever you have set yourself the task of finding.

It seems to me that dowsing, the ability to *search and find*, is an intuitive part of all human beings, and is also a basic component of the survival mechanism of *all* the many other species, which are a part of our biosphere.

Therefore, dowsing is an essential factor in the evolution of all life.

Surely, it follows that it would be an excellent idea to incorporate the art of dowsing into any system of education, aimed at increasing the abilities of the young and broadening the horizons of their minds.

A few years ago, with the aid of my friend and colleague, Terry Steele, a skilled and open-minded television and film director, we gave a demonstration of this ability, with the help of four eleven-year-old children, two boys and two girls.

Terry invited me to a plant nursery, near Reading, where, the night before, he had arranged for a long hose-pipe to be hidden, some six inches below the ground, which was then raked over to remove any signs of soil disturbance.

In front of the cameras and the amused television crew, I then gave the children, none of whom I had met before, a few minutes' instruction in the use of dowsers' angle-rods. These are three-foot lengths of coat-hanger wire bent into an 'L' shape, the shorter arms of the wires being held in the fingers of each hand, at waist-height, with the longer arms pointing forwards and parallel to the ground.

I explained to the children, who were very bright, that they were to walk slowly over the selected piece of ground and, when they felt the rods move in their fingers, apparently of their own accord, they were to stop, and place a marker into the earth.

We gave six of these markers, which were plastic windmills on sticks, to each child, whom we now positioned, at intervals, along the raked area of ground.

The youngsters entered into the spirit of the experiment, and, because they were relaxed and having fun, without suffering from any blocking of their minds by doubt or nervousness, they gave an impressive demonstration of their natural dowsing ability.

The line of children had been stationed, unknown to them, parallel with the buried hosepipe. This had been laid in a serpentine shape, the total length of the pipe being some fifty yards.

The well-raked soil showed no sign of disturbance and the only evidence of the presence of the buried hose was the stand-pipe at one end and a damp spot at the other end of the prepared ground, where the water had seeped out. However, there was no way that any of us, using our normal faculties, could have detected the exact course of the buried hose-pipe.

At a signal from Terry, the children moved forward, planting their little windmills into the soil, whenever their angle-rods rotated in their fingers.

The television crew were intrigued and silently watched the slow progress of the children, while they marked out a long serpentine pattern on the ground.

This snake-like marking was the work of three of the children, the two girls and one of the boys. The other lad marched straight across the prepared ground and planted six of his windmills, in a straight line, about fifteen yards long and parallel to a glass greenhouse.

'Three out of four isn't bad for an off-the-cuff demonstration, with untried children,' I whispered to Terry, who nodded his agreement.

We reached the end of the experiment, when the youngsters ran out of windmills.

'Right!' said my director. 'Now let's see what we've got.'

With the aid of the crew and in full view of the cameras, we pulled hard on the stand-pipe end of the hose-pipe and carefully followed its course, as we forced the hose to come up through the soil.

To everyone's amazement, the pipe appeared directly *under each one* of the windmills.

I certainly didn't want to embarrass the one child who, demonstrably, had got it wrong.

'That was pretty conclusive!' I said. 'Of course, we can't all expect to get it right, first time.'

At this point, the nurseryman, who had been an astonished witness to the experiment, walked into camera range, and, with his face red with excitement, blurted out, 'The lad didn't get it wrong. He marked the bloody main!'

It was a shame about the word 'bloody', because we couldn't use this startling statement in a children's programme. But there was no doubt in anyone's mind that the experiment had been a great success.

Those children had picked up the principle behind dowsing in a few minutes. Why then do we not teach our children skills like this, in our schools, when the aborigines of Australia do so, as well as the Bedouin who teach their children to find water as a matter of basic survival? Add to these the Hottentots and Bushmen of the Kalahari and other tribesmen of the more arid parts of Africa. For them all, dowsing in various forms is a vital part of their children's education. Yet we totally ignore the teaching of this art to our children with the excuse of thinking of it as mumbo-jumbo or a form of witchcraft and a useless waste of time.

Yet many of those children would thoroughly enjoy this exciting game, and dowsing has many applications, including finding the way home if one becomes lost. Surely that quality alone makes it worth while teaching in our schools. I cannot believe that our splendid teachers are so close-minded that they would object to experienced dowsers demonstrating their art.

Those ten years of experiment and research into dowsing have taught me the fundamentals of this exciting art.

How does it work?

So far, nobody really knows for certain, but the most logical explanation, as I mentioned earlier, seems to be the one provided by Professor Tiller's theory that biological antennae, formed by the body's combined nervous systems, enables the brain to transmit and receive signals of extremely low frequency, ranging from half a Hertz to approximately 100 Hertz (cycles per second).

He has also published a thought-provoking paper:

'The possibility of the existence of biological antennae in the human body, capable of the transmission and reception of very low frequencies.' Apparently the tremendous length of antennae required for this to occur, is more than served by the aggregate potential length of the body's combined nervous systems, which I understand from an anatomist can be of the staggering order of some 600,000 kilometres!

That evidently is made up of the total of all the microscopic hair-like filaments of the cillae, plus the neurones, dendrites, axons and synapses, which make up the incredible complexity of our nervous systems.

This might well explain why in all religions and cult-practices, the officiating priest, imams, rabbis, hierophants, or shamans, appear to orientate themselves, by first facing the four cardinal points of the compass, usually while raising the arms, rather as though they themselves were a dipole aerial.

This also could account for the detection of the presence of subterranean water, buried cables and gas-pipes, or the finding of mineral deposits and the marking out, on the surface, of the shape of underground chambers etc. by the dowser using the hands alone, without employing any other indicator. The dowser's hands are part of the body's biological antennae system, and react to anomalies in weak energy fields, detected in the earth beneath.

To some extent this is being borne out by the somewhat crude instruments, now being developed by gas and electricity companies, which, when operated by their respective engineers, synthesize similar, but far less accurate, results to those obtained by the experienced dowsers that all these organizations also use.

This is yet another example of how all the instrumentation that we develop is only an extension of our own natural abilities!

However, it doesn't offer a facile explanation for the other remarkable ability of dowsers and diviners to detect the location of objects or persons, alive or dead, at great distances, by swinging their pendulums over large-scale charts of the area, where the missing subjects of the search were last seen, or were thought to have been located.

Many investigators, usually self-appointed, with their bigotry evident in their arrogance, dismiss all the huge mass of evidence out-of-hand, and, if they do conduct cursory experiments, treat the dowsers involved with rudeness and condescension, thereby creating a negative and hostile atmosphere, in sharp contrast to the required objectivity, needed to research paranormal phenomena properly.

No artist can work, or operate, within such a negative ambience, and therefore, the results tend only to confirm the so-called researchers' already damning attitude, turning such experiments into an embarrassing farce.

Please remember that, in all the fields of the paranormal, we are dealing, essentially, with an art, in one form or another, and artists, of all kinds, are, by their nature, extremely sensitive to atmosphere. None of them object to a fair-minded assessment of their abilities, but few seldom get such courteous treatment.

One of the most prominent figures, in this kind of investigation, is the self-proclaimed 'Amazing Randi', who has made quite a reputation for himself in the sensational press.

This immodest showman claims to be the doyen of 'Psychic Investigators', specializing in the exposure of fraudulent practices. From his self-description I cannot see much objectivity in his approach to this research. My friend Paul Daniels, the famous TV magician, for whom I predicted an outstanding success when we were working together many years ago in a summer season in Jersey, has told me that he finds dowsing particularly to be a valid phenomenon which he can't explain, especially when he tried it for himself.

So has another friend, David Berglass, who like Paul is a first-class stage magician with a deep knowledge of all the tricks of the trade. David believes that, when the phenomenon is not fully explicable, in the terms of 'stage magic', we are evidently dealing with the powers of the human mind which science, so far, has not yet fully researched.

Nevertheless, both these skilled and popular magicians, in common with all good professional performers, must have a long personal experience of stage nerves, and, therefore, I am sure they both appreciate that the subject of these tests and examinations can be adversely affected, if the experimental conditions are hostile.

For these skilled stage magicians, as for me, a full explanation of genuine paranormal phenomena is still to be found by qualified, open-minded scientists. Like my father, I believe that it is because we are dealing with an art form, that, up till now, no one, scientist or art critic, has been able to accurately measure, quantify or qualify, any form of art other than as a matter of personal preference, or opinion.

To give you a hypothetical example of what I mean: suppose that we are evaluating the art of two great actors, by the same methods currently in vogue with scientific paranormal investigation.

We select two leading exponents of this art, say Sir Alec Guinness and Miss Meryl Streep, and test them, using the scientific methods, currently in vogue, to test sensitives, to determine whether they can perform the famous scene between Macbeth and Lady Macbeth by William Shakespeare.

In pursuance of these scientific methods, we first enclose them in a metal Faraday cage, to make certain that they are not receiving outside radio transmissions, on some hidden instrument. Then we strip them both and submit them to an impertinent and thorough body search, to see whether they have any other apparatus concealed about their persons.

We next attach various prosthetic devices to their heads and bodies, to measure their brain-waves, pulse-rates, respiration, skin-resistance and other electro-chemical activity. We then tell them to proceed with their scene from *Macbeth*.

If they were willing to continue to act under these uncomfortable conditions, these two splendid practitioners of their art would undoubtedly do the best they could, because they are both supreme professionals, but I doubt whether they would be giving their best performances. Would the scientific investigators then conclude that neither Sir Alec Guinness, nor Miss Meryl Streep, were very convincing in these famous roles, and, consequently, that they were both *fraudulent* practitioners of the art of acting?

Certainly that would be the case, if the subjects under investigation were engaged in contemporary tests to ascertain their validity as practitioners of a paranormal art form, such as dowsing, or other kinds of mediumship.

That is another reason why I must reiterate the importance of the artistic concept of the paranormal, because it helps to make sense out of the maze of contradictory explanations of this whole field of human experience.

If you are an artist yourself, you will already be familiar with the one-day-on, one-day-off nature of the arts and know just how erratic these abilities can be. You will also know, only too well, how a negative atmosphere can interfere, drastically, with the practice of your art, no matter in which field of creativity you are involved.

The well-known comedian, Jerry Lewis, once told me that, in his long experience, he had found comedy to be such a fragile thing where atmosphere is concerned, and that having just one person in a film crew projecting an 'I suppose you think that's funny' attitude, was quite sufficient to destroy a whole scene. Furthermore, if the person concerned continued to work on the film, he or she could affect, adversely, the comedy of the entire movie. Jerry Lewis also told me that conversely the same, deleterious effect, could be generated on the movie set if the comedian surrounded himself with sycophants who laughed at everything he did.

My own experience, in over forty-one years of comedy in television, films, stage and cabaret work completely bears out this clever performer's perceptive statement.

It emphasizes how powerful the force of negative thinking can be.

In cabaret, where the performer is frequently confronted by loud-mouthed drunks and the arrogant hostility of those who want to be noticed, there is to be found a good, if unpleasant, training ground for performers, especially when their bread-and-butter depends on their success.

The late Danny Kaye, who was a superb performer, once told me that he dreaded that type of disturbance when working with an audience, because it felt to him like a blow to the solar plexus.

In fact, no matter how professionally hardened and experienced the artist may be, he or she takes a moment to recover, after such an attack. Even the best ad-libbers in show business, who specialize in 'put-down' gags, as they are called, and who are capable of destroying the most vicious and persistent hecklers, still find this sort of situation a strain, and one that he or she could do without.

The list of famous artists, with whom I have discussed the same thing, is long, and I have never found one, even among the toughest and most hardened performers, who did not feel the same way about heckling in cabaret.

Consequently, anybody involved in the practice of an art or craft, in which total concentration and a high degree of sensitivity is involved, will be affected in a similar manner, and this applies equally to those who are demonstrating the paranormal abilities of their minds.

Moreover, the same rules apply to those who are training animals to exert their extrasensory powers, as in the case of tracker dogs.

Policemen and members of mountain rescue-teams have told me that a similar negative mental attitude in the treatment of their dogs and blood-hounds, can affect adversely to a marked degree, the normally remarkable performance of these animals.

Let us return to dowsing, as a demonstrable art, and consider it as a remnant of the survival-senses of our distant ancestors which we can utilize in many ways.

I hosted and chaired the 1985-6 International Dowsing Conference at Oxford University for three days and I met and discussed with delegates, from all over the world, the range of these talents in both humans and animals.

During the conference we had to speak a number of languages to communicate with these interesting people, whose professions covered the whole spectrum of the arts and sciences. Engineers, military, naval and airforce personnel, including generals, and senior officers of many countries, scientists, architects, surveyors, engineers, mathematicians, medical men, surgeons, and people from every walk of life, all agreed that dowsing was a valid part of their lives and a welcome aid in backing up their everyday judgement, even in medical diagnosis.

Therefore, I have no hesitation in recommending that the reader should try to find out more about this fascinating subject, beyond the brief outline that I offer in this book. I promise that, for the open-minded reader, this will be a worthwhile experience.

The books that I recommend you read, before you decide whether or not to contact the British or American Society of Dowsers, for further help and information, are first, *Dowsing*, by Tom Graves, (available from Watkins bookstore, 19-21 Cecil Court, Charing Cross Road, London, W1). This is an excellent, profusely illustrated book, which provides a lucid and easy-to-follow guide for anyone who wishes to find out if they can dowse. Secondly, I recommend *Pattern of the Past*, by Guy Underwood (also available from the same source). The late author has written a fascinating survey of his own dowsing experiences, with particular attention to his theories about why the stone circles of the British Isles and other ancient structures on sacred sites were built and how their form and situation affects their environment and those who visit them.

You may not agree with the author, but it will stimulate you to try dowsing these sites for yourself, and you may be surprised by the results. I certainly was!

Also read any of the books by Tom Lethbridge which deal with dowsing. (Again, a list of his works, all eminently readable, can be obtained from Watkins bookstore, which I recommend, because I live near London and the proprietors are always most helpful.)

Lethbridge was an antiquarian, at Cambridge University, and his remarkable researches resulted, among other things, in the discovery by dowsing and the eventual restoration of two prehistoric giant earth-figures, 'Gog' and 'Magog', cut into the landscape, but hidden under the grass in East Anglia.

This extraordinary man was an explorer, a sailor of small boats to remote places, an archaeologist and all-round scholar, and his open-minded works are excellent foci for anyone wishing to find a firm base from which to tackle research into the entrancing world of dowsing. Colin Wilson also recommends Tom Lethbridge's work, unreservedly.

This short list will do for the time being, to start you off.

There are, of course, many other valid and interesting works on the same subject by Colonel Scott-Elliott, Sir William Barratt, the Abbé Mermet, Henri de France, *et al*. But, for a sound and attention-holding introduction to dowsing, you can't better the first three authors. I know you will enjoy their books.

At least, dowsing will get you and probably your family, as well, out into the fresh air, perhaps looking for so-called 'Leys' and 'Ley lines', or exploring ancient sites, and, at best, this art, which is most probably inherent in all of us, will open up a new vista of life, both past and present, on our planet.

It will also make serious practitioners aware of the role they can play, in improving the present, lamentable state of most of our civilized world.

To give you a rough overview of what dowsers can sense, by using their art, let me take you through some of the successes, achieved by various notable practitioners.

Bill Lewis, another friend, with great experience in dowsing, has produced results, which cannot be explained by that word which is over-used by sceptics: coincidence.

At the Oxford Conference, he showed me a number of press-cuttings, dealing with his location, by remote-dowsing, of a sunken fishing-vessel, which had gone down under unusual circumstances, without the crew having had time to send a Mayday distress call. Bill was only called in, after a number of attempts had been made by an Admiralty salvage team to find the site of the sinking, which was, apparently, one of a number of other *similar* fishing-vessels lost, without warning. The British Admiralty were very concerned, because their department of Marine Architecture has to approve the building of all such vessels, and their loss could have been due to a basic fault in their design or construction.

Working from large-scale charts, sent to him by the Naval Salvage experts, Bill Lewis pinpointed the position of the wreck so accurately, that the Royal Navy diver was reported as having landed on the deck of the sunken vessel.

In the Abbé Mermet's book, you will find a long list of attested cases of the famous dowser-priest having located many missing persons, alive or dead, using remote-dowsing techniques, with large-scale charts and his pendulum.

How was it then, that I could not employ the same methods to find my own missing son, in 1971?

At that time, I had not met Colin Bloy and his associates, and I had only the vaguest knowledge of what dowsing was about and what dowsers could and could not do. I only met Colin in 1976, after a programme about my life had been shown on television. He wrote to me, suggesting that we could mutually benefit from a meeting – which is exactly what happened.

I am very grateful to both Colin and his brother David, and all the other friendly dowsers who so kindly showed me, without regard for their time or effort, how skilfully they practised their art.

Let us consider some of the different techniques by which dowsers tune themselves in to their unconscious minds and, as I believe, to the collective unconscious (the universal overmind), as well.

In the case of the traditional water-diviner, to use a popular term, the dowser uses a light, springy, forked twig cut from a hazel tree, willow, or any other suitable source of 'Y'-shaped branches. Holding the forked branch in the fingers of both hands, with the pointed end of the 'Y' in front, the dowser adjusts the pressure on the twig exerted by the fingers and the position of the wrists, until the twig is meta-stable. That is to say, the twig is under balanced tension and torsion, to a degree that it can move freely, either way, up or down, by rotating in the dowser's fingers.

However, this sudden rotation will only occur when the small musculature in the fingers reacts to the dowser's unconscious mental responses, as he, or she, detects the presence of the underground stream, or whatever is being sought.

Some dowsers like to hold the fork palm upwards, and others prefer to work with their palms pointing down. It is purely a matter of choice.

The twig's movement is similar to the response of the needle on a sensitive potentiometer, when the instrument detects the presence of a current of electricity, and causes the needle to swing round a dial.

That is all the process entails, so far as a witness to this type of dowsing is concerned.

However, from the dowser's point of view, the process is somewhat different. I will describe it in its simplest form.

The *first* rotation of the twig, upwards or downwards, according to the way it is held, takes place, as the dowser walks slowly over the 'outer-marker', or outer 'water-line', as it is called, indicating the presence of an underground stream, or spring, in the area.

The *second* reaction of the forked twig, as the dowser continues walking, tells him, or her, that below that exact spot lies the course of the stream, or the location of the spring. Furthermore, by continuing to walk and dowse, yet another reaction will soon be found.

The distance between the *second* reaction, where the spring was located and this *final* one, indicates at what depth the water is located.

This is known as: 'The Bishop's Rule'.

Of course, I am making this short introduction to the art of dowsing ridiculously simplistic. But, in essence, it is simple and its practice is a question of the individual dowser's skill and experience.

The course of an underground stream, or spring, its rate of flow, the purity of the water, and even its predicted mineral content are all within the divining capabilities of a good dowser, with considerable experience.

But there is nothing mystical about it. It is basically the 'search and find' capability of the human and animal mind.

I have seen remarkable demonstrations of these capabilities, and Central Television has made a fascinating programme about one of my dowsing friends, Roy Talbot, who divined the exact position of subterranean water for a farmer, and then following the course of the subsequent drilling and the bringing-in of the well, precisely where my dowser friend had predicted that it would be.

Moreover, he also, accurately, predicted the depth at which the stream was located, its purity, and its exact rate of flow.

It was altogether a mind-boggling experience, which, naturally, was ignored by the technological Establishment, to whom it would have been an embarrassment, because they could not have explained how it was done, in the light of their present state of knowledge.

Therefore, as far as they were concerned, it must have been a trick, an illusion, made possible by the collusion of the television company, the farmer and the dowser, all of whom instantly were suspected of being involved in a fraudulent demonstration.

That seems to be the main block to genuine research into the field of extrasensory perception.

The technologists, feeling themselves threatened by such a situation, which they cannot, from their position of professional expertise, adequately explain in terms of contemporary technology, turn their backs on such experiments and prefer to ignore them, rather than to investigate their validity.

The dowser uses a number of different indicators, which act as the needle for the potentiometer of his or her mind, and all these simple methods and techniques work well.

Whether they consist of using a springy forked twig, two 'L'-shaped pieces of coat-hanger wire, a spiral spring, held under tension by a handle on either end, or a pendulum, swung from the thumb and first finger of either hand, is entirely up to the dowser's personal preference.

That they do work is undeniable, at least as far as I am concerned, and I am only one among many witnesses who later became practitioners.

Actually, a very experienced dowser, eventually, can do the same things, without using any of these indicators, and practise the art by the use of his, or her, hands alone.

I have seen that done a number of times. But the dowser, Colin Bloy, was very experienced and had practised his art, to a remarkable degree.

So, once again, after over ten years' research into the art of dowsing, I have come to the conclusion that this is within the range of most people's ability, provided they keep an open mind and entertain no doubts whatsoever, while engaged in its practice.

But then, after all, that proviso also applies to any difficult undertaking, from drawing, painting, sculpture, composition, poetry, writing, practising the art of medicine or surgery, creative engineering, or chemistry, multi-dimensional mathematics, or any other form of creative thinking, to driving an untried racing-car, test-flying an experimental plane, or being engaged in any original project, where doubt will only hamper, not help, the operation.

All imaginative and creative pursuits, which are expressly aimed at widening the horizons of our knowledge of ourselves, and the universe around us, must be subject to those cardinal rules:

(1) Open the mind.
(2) Listen to the voice of intuition.
(3) Filter the result through the process of rationale.

They are also the rules that my father taught me, fifty-five years ago.

How then, does all this affect the issue of leaving the earth in the state, or even in a better state, than you would wish to find it?

The answer is simple.

Once you become aware of how closely you are bound into the cycles of our planet's ecology, and sense how much a part of the earth you really are, the more you will cherish the sanctity of our 'Whole System', (ecos and ethos), and do your utmost to preserve its *status quo*, in as healthy a state and condition as possible.

Therefore, you will become reluctant to add to the appalling pollution of our world, which is being carried

137

out in the name of profit, and you will feel strongly motivated to do something about it.

This also applies to the mental pollution of our ethos, which is as serious a problem as the poisoning of our environment, for both these actions are *crimes against humanity*, and, especially, against the future health and welfare of our posterity.

Only by opening our minds to the dangers of this situation and seeking the aid of our fellows in banding together to combat these threats to our continued existence, can we and our children survive.

I believe that dowsing is one of the many ways to open our minds, to become more aware of our real potential and that of the whole of humanity, in a proper relationship to the rest of *all* life on this earth.

Therefore, I strongly recommend that you should investigate, as I did, the validity, or otherwise, of the art of dowsing.

CHAPTER SEVEN

Open your mind to healing

How valid is healing? That is like asking: How valid is any other art?

Even the most bigoted physician, or surgeon, will admit that medicine and surgery are both arts and that there are times when he, or she, makes a mistaken diagnosis of a patient's condition, even when backed-up by the present sophisticated state of knowledge amassed in the archives of these two great practices.

In the now outmoded Hippocratic oath, which, until recently, all newly-qualified doctors and surgeons swore, as a matter of course, the words: 'Practise my Art' were clearly stated.

Therefore, when a lay-person correctly diagnoses the condition of a patient and pinpoints the location of the trauma, malfunction, or disease and accurately defines the condition, and its pathology, and goes on to describe, rather than prescribe (which is the province of a qualified doctor) the correct treatment for that condition; surely, the medical profession should, at least, show some interest in the validity, or otherwise, of the genuine healer's strange abilities, and not just condemn it all, out of hand.

This has been a situation which I have witnessed many times during the course of my life.

Because of these unusual experiences, after allowing for the factors of chance and coincidence, even to a degree beyond reasonable mathematical calculation, there has been more than sufficient evidence to convince me of the validity of healing, outside the range of the accepted arts of medicine and surgery.

It is only recently, that the study of psychosomatic medicine has been given approval by members of the two professions, and that I have had the opportunity, during my fund-raising efforts on behalf of cancer research, to talk to a number of distinguished practitioners, about their attitudes towards it. What they have told me further strengthens my belief that the power of the mind has a direct bearing on a patient's state of health, and that his, or her, confidence in a valid healer can be of great benefit especially if the patient is suffering from a terminal condition.

Confidence is also vital in the relationship between conventional doctors or surgeons and their patients. A number of highly-qualified practitioners have told me that their 'bedside' manner is as important, in its way, as a physician's or surgeon's academic qualifications and practical experience.

The Bible quotation: 'Physician heal thyself' has great validity in another context: it is the patient, through the immune system of the body and the power of the mind who actually does the healing. In many of the cases I have known, especially in wartime, the patient though gravely wounded made the final decision to live or die. This became apparent to me when visiting badly-wounded or seriously-ill friends, who were determined to survive, while others less grievously hurt died, presumably because they could not summon up the will to live.

Many friends, who are doctors, have told me much the same story.

That is why I am so keen on the concept of whollistic healing, which is the art of healing the *whole person*. I am also in disagreement with the present practice of spelling the word Whollistic, as Holistic, because this implies a mystical meaning, and tends to bring religion into the equation.

While I do not wish to interfere with any person's religious beliefs, I feel that this idea of something holy being involved in the art of healing, immediately brings the established churches into the matter, and, for me, the practice of the art of healing should apply as much to atheists, and agnostics, as to conventional believers.

In other words: it should be a universal art, for *anyone* capable of its practice, irrespective of race, colour, creed or religion.

Having said this, let me give you some idea of the sort of healing that I have witnessed, or have been told about, first hand, while it was happening, or soon after it had happened.

During the many years that I worked with my father, I saw some remarkable demonstrations of healing, many being practised by Pop himself.

These instances ranged from successful treatments of conditions which, even to my young mind, were being aggravated by the subject's disturbed state of mind, to actual physical benefits, such as the regaining of hearing for a deaf person, or obviously improved movement of the limbs, in the cases of those who had been partially paralysed, and the evident relief from pain and suffering of those afflicted by various serious conditions.

In almost all the cases to which I am referring, the person involved had been 'given-up' (I use their own words) by the medical and surgical professions, as *incurable*. That is not a melodramatic statement, written for effect, but rather the facts, as I knew them at the time.

Some of these unfortunate people were suffering from conditions which had been partially, or wholly, induced by hysteria and, presumably, their confidence in the healers who were treating them was the determining factor in their subsequent healing.

Whether their conditions were alleviated by the transfer of some form of energy emanating from the healers, or were caused by radical changes in their own mental condition at the time, the results – which for me are what count the most – were remarkable.

Certainly, as a youngster and later as an adult, I have witnessed more than enough cases of seemingly miraculous healing, to convince me that genuine, as opposed to self-deluded, healers can work wonders, where, often, conventional medical practitioners have failed to effect a cure, temporary or otherwise.

One of the most remarkable of these healers, with whom I had personal dealings, was Eddie Partridge, the grocer from Dover in whom Pop had every confidence. His most rewarding case of almost instantaneous healing bears repeating. I got the story first-hand from my father when he returned home the same night.

Apparently, Pop and Eddie had been discussing a forthcoming sitting that they had arranged, with the intention of helping a case of Possession, (the apparent take-over of a person's body by another personality).

Suddenly, the shop door of Eddie's small store in Dover burst open and in rushed a young girl, weeping hysterically. The poor child, who was about twelve years old, was very pretty, but she was suffering from severe acne, which, at her tender age, must have been torture for her.

'I'm going to throw myself over the cliff, Uncle Eddie!' she sobbed, as she hugged her comforting friend who was much loved by all the children in the neighbourhood.

'No! you're not, dear,' replied Eddie, gently soothing the hysterical girl.

'You go back home to your mum and have a lie-down. I promise you, dear, everything is going to be all right! You'll see!'

As he spoke, Eddie passed his hand lightly over the girl's face, as though he was wiping away the dreadful, disfiguring condition.

Instantly, the young girl stopped crying, as Eddie's calm certainty that she would be all right reassured her, and

142

she quietly left the shop and returned home, her former hysteria completaly gone.

'That in itself was a minor miracle,' my father told us. 'I felt so sorry for that poor lass. She was such a pretty girl and that appalling acne had ruined her complexion.' He paused, shaking his head. 'But, what happened next is beyond any logical explanation!'

Apparently, about an hour or so after this incident, the same girl rushed excitedly into the shop.

'Look at me, Uncle Eddie!' she cried, her face radiant with happiness.

Pop told us that he could hardly believe the extraordinary change in the girl's complexion.

There virtually was not a mark on her face!

The many ugly, red blotches and suppurating spots had completely disappeared, leaving no sign whatsoever of what had been an extremely bad case of acne.

'It really was a miracle!' he said and added, 'I'm sure the last time anything like this happened, the healer wasn't a grocer from Dover, but a carpenter from Nazareth!'

My father was not being blasphemous. He was just trying to find an adequate simile to fit the miraculous event.

I have never forgotten how impressed Pop was, by that particular piece of healing.

'You should have seen the look on that pretty child's face, as she looked at Eddie. It was the pure look of love that one associates with Bible stories about Jesus, and His special relationship with children.'

I remember thinking, at the time, how unlike my father's usual dispassionate, objective and scientific viewpoint that statement was.

Since then, both my father and I discussed this case with a number of interested scientists and medical men, and heard some bizarre explanations of this remarkable healing.

'Obviously, fraud!' said one complacent physician. 'The child evidently was a consummate actress and had deliberately disfigured herself. She probably used her mother's make-up to fake the acne.'

Now there's a sensible theory! It presumes that a twelve-year-old girl has an acting skill, comparable with Shirley Temple's outstanding childhood ability, plus a skill in make-up that would have taxed the ability of a top cosmetic technician, specializing in horror movies.

Another more ingenious, but still unlikely explanation, was that the girl was an identical twin, who suffered from dreadful acne, while her sister was unmarked. Both of them, presumably, were playing a macabre trick on their much-loved friend.

This theory also failed to convince us, because, as Eddie had explained to my father, the girl was an only child of an unhappy marriage, which was why he had been so concerned that the hysterical girl really might have done something drastic, like jumping off the Dover cliffs.

However, a third explanation does bear more careful consideration. This one was given me by a psychiatrist, who was a Roman Catholic.

'In my religion,' he said, 'there are many authenticated cases of *religious ecstasy* resulting in the appearance of what we call "stigmata". This type of physical phenomenon seems to duplicate the appearance of the wounds of Jesus Christ, which we believe He suffered, during His Crucifixion.

'However, this sort of hysterically-induced trauma usually manifests among deeply religious priests, nuns, or monks, who are often members of closed, or contemplative Orders, and one of the most recent examples has been that of Father Pia, a dedicated Italian priest. But, it is most unusual for stigmata to occur among lay-persons. However, there have been rare cases of this kind happening among the laity.'

Such cases have been widely reported and authenticated throughout the history of the Roman Catholic faith, but, in every instance, the phenomenon of stigmata has appeared, as a facsimile of *the wounds of Christ*.

But I have never heard of a case of hysterically-induced acne appearing and, what is more important, completely *disappearing* so quickly, apparently, without leaving a single mark, when it is usual for such an unsightly dermatological condition to leave some scarring or pitting on the skin of the sufferer.

However, what mattered to my father and to me, was that Eddie Partridge had succeeded in healing every trace of that appalling disfigurement, *in a little over an hour*.

That was undeniable!

From the time that my father and mother became deeply involved in research into paranormal phenomena, I met a long succession of psychics, mediums, sensitives and healers.

Many were self-deluded, quite a few were downright charlatans, but, wonderfully, a precious nucleus of fascinating folk turned out to be genuine practitioners of their remarkable art.

These were the ones who formed the solid foundation for my belief in the ability of certain gifted people to pass on the benefit of their healing ability to others.

In the case of the *genuine* sensitives, whom we knew personally, whether they were clairvoyants, clairaudients, psychometrists, transfiguration mediums, like Mrs Enid Balmer, or telekinetics, with the demonstrable ability to affect the movement of heavy objects, or other kinds of physical mediums, capable of manifesting 'Direct Voice' and 'Materialization' phenomena; many of them seemed to have the extra ability to heal, in varying degrees of effectiveness.

In fact, it seemed to my father, my brother and myself, that their psychic abilities often gave them the additional power to practise healing, or, at least, to channel some kind of beneficial energy to those who needed it.

Just as with their paranormal sensitivity, their ability to heal also seemed to vary, at different times, so, evidently, many diverse factors were involved in the practice of this art, as well.

During those many years, in peace and war, it became clear that the basic energies, involved in healing, were positive. Any *negative* thoughts or destructive attitudes tended to stop, or even *to reverse* the healing process.

Taking into consideration the fact that human beings, and for that matter all living beings on the planet, are electro-chemical by nature, then obviously, whatever the process of healing may be, it must be electro-chemical in origin.

Thought itself is a manifestation of the same electro-chemical energy, whether the process of thinking is generated consciously or unconsciously and, from the evidence I have witnessed and assessed in over fifty years of research, positive thinking appears to be able to overcome negative thinking. Therefore I believe that most healing is the result of the healer's own positive thinking, or if you prefer it, complete faith, causing a beneficial reaction in the recipient's immune systems, thereby reinforcing their own built-in system of self-healing.

An outstanding example of another application of the extraordinary power of positive thinking was the outcome of one particular battle, during the Second World War. For me, and for millions of thinking men and women, the outcome of the Battle of Britain, in which the numerically far smaller Royal Air Force defeated the much larger and more battle-experienced German Luftwaffe, was a miracle!

Our opponents had already been blooded in Spain, Poland, Norway, Holland, Belgium and France, and the Battle itself was an inspiring demonstration of what the collective human spirit can do, when aroused and self-dedicated to a common cause.

In 1940, I was still an eighteen-year-old civilian during that bitter struggle to prevent the German invasion of Britain throughout that long summer, but, like so many other young men and women, I was able to participate and help, as a member of the civilian auxiliary services, in my case, in the ARP (Air Raid Precautions).

146

During that grim, but strangely stimulating time, I saw the whole nation united in its efforts to stave off the rape of the British Isles.

Scottish, Welsh, Irish and English, whether male or female, young or old, Protestant, Catholic, Non-Conformist, Jewish, Muslim, Hindu, or Buddhist, atheist, agnostic or Deist, everyone seemed to forget their religious and ethnic differences and their political credos. They joined together, in single-minded positive thinking, to throw back the evil menace of the Nazis.

From the moment that Winston Churchill took over the leadership of a beleaguered Britain, and told Parliament and the people, in simple unequivocal terms, what we faced as a nation, the whole country seemed to become transformed into a determined, armed camp.

I still remember my mother's reaction to the news of Churchill taking over the premiership: 'We are going to be all right now. The bloody-minded old bulldog is back!'

That staunch old soldier's key words to Parliament were contained in the famous motion that he proposed, in the House of Commons: 'That this House is not interested in the possibility of defeat.'

The typically Churchillian phrase seemed to capture the public mood. Without question the public accepted their new leader's offer: 'Blood, Toil, Tears and Sweat.'

Then the island people managed to snatch from the beaches of Dunkirk and carry back to Britain some 340,000 of the besieged British and Allied soldiers, many of whom were rescued by British amateur yachtsmen in their small boats, most of which had never before left the Thames.

Meanwhile, back home, everyone applied themselves to the task of re-arming and training themselves to win the war.

Almost immediately, Churchill, through the religious leaders of all the different churches in Britain, irrespective of their denomination, called for a day of national

147

prayer. I well remember joining in that first concentrated, mass outpouring of *positive thinking*, as the British people, together with their Commonwealth friends, and their Allies, French, Belgian, Dutch, Czech, Polish and Norwegian, concentrated on healing their wounds, both material and spiritual, and prayed for victory.

Those terrible wounds were many!

First, there had been the near-extermination of the British Expeditionary Force and the remnants of its French, Dutch and Belgian Allies on the beaches of Dunkirk. Those exhausted soldiers had been saved by a seeming miracle, involving the total effort of the Royal Navy and a few Allied ships, reinforced by that extraordinary cockleshell fleet, manned by lifeboatmen, British merchant sailors and amateur yachtsmen.

Secondly, Britain had lost many men and ships, with almost all the vital material of war in the disastrous Norwegian campaign, which had ended in total defeat for the Northern Allied Expeditionary Force.

Thirdly, death and dreadful wounds were being inflicted, by day and by night, on the civilian population, from the round-the-clock bombing of Britain, in the air war, which became known as the 'Battle of Britain'.

These vital air battles were under the command of the sensitive and open-minded Air Marshal Sir Hugh Dowding, a friend of my father's who, like Pop, for many years had been engaged in the investigation of the Paranormal.

Those days of national prayer, or positive thinking, which were called for by Winston Churchill continued throughout the entire war. The nation prayed together whenever the Allied cause was faced with dire defeat and dreadful losses. This outpouring of positive thinking also provided a source of healing for the 'Volk-Geist', as the Germans called it, the 'spirit' of Britain, and those of her Allies, and renewed our determination to win the war against the Nazis.

To me, and I am sure to many others, it seemed as though here was the greatest demonstration of both mass healing and positive thinking ever undertaken by a nation and its Allies.

The ringing of churchbells had been forbidden during the first few years of the war, because this was the agreed signal to the people of Britain, that the German invasion of our island had begun. In these silenced churches, the voices of the packed congregations of all denominations were raised in song, or quietly engaged in their prayers for victory, and for the safety of their loved ones. From personal experience, I can say that these wartime church services were one of the most moving experiences of my life.

I believe, along with a lot of others, that those commonly shared mystical experiences, like massed prayers or intense comradeship were the main reasons why those who remember the war, cannot recapture that extraordinary positive spirit, which bound us all together in that single, mighty purpose. Only occasionally, today, among all the division and dissension often deliberately induced by militant extremists, do we catch a hint of what that great sense of purpose was all about.

The 'Last Night of the Proms', that annual joyous finale at the Albert Hall which marks the end of the Promenade concerts, seems to generate something of the same unique spirit of those grim days, when Britain stood alone against the seemingly invincible Axis and the Powers of Darkness. Is this just an over-dramatization by someone who remembers the terrible days of the Second World War?

I don't think so, for many young people who make up the bulk of the audience watching the 'Last Night of the Proms' in that great Victorian concert hall, or viewing the concert on television, feel that same elusive sense of unity and many of them have remarked upon it.

That joyous musical event, full of youthful enthusiasm and energy, is a perfect example of what I mean by the healing power of positive thinking.

Just to listen to it makes you feel good!

When I talk, or write, about my belief in the existence of the power of healing, I am referring to a source of energy which I believe comes from the vast amount of free electrons within the confines of the ionospheric vault surrounding the earth, coupled with the ability of genuine healers to transfer this power through the channel of their bodies, via their nervous systems which act as antenae, to the recipient who is in need of healing.

I am also convinced, by my experience of these wartime outpourings of the power of national unity, that positive energy from the same source can be generated by people's concentrated mass prayer, i.e. positive thinking, and that this energy, similarly, can be channelled through them to benefit a community, a nation, or even the whole world.

Certainly, His Holiness, Pope John Paul II, demonstrably, shares the same belief.

The attempted assassination of the Pope, when he was struck by several 9mm bullets, fired from a high-powered automatic pistol, including one bullet that pierced his abdomen, is a case for the existence of the power of mass prayer.

This extraordinary man, who was born in Poland, was, as a young boy, an active member of the Polish Resistance at the time of the Warsaw uprising. So the Pope understood what violence was all about when, at the age of sixty, that unforgivable assassination attempt was made against him. Yet, his immediate reaction, amid the agony of his wounds, apart from shock and surprise that anyone should do such a thing, was to *forgive* his murderous assailant. That is the act of a truly remarkable man!

Thousands of his admirers and staunch supporters were in the close vicinity, and most of them gladly would have risked their lives to stop the assassin, had that been possible.

Through the medium of the television screen, viewers all over the world could feel the shock and horror that surrounded this evil act. Those pictures of the thousands of people who were present, kneeling on the hard cobbles and praying fervently that His Holiness might live, will stay with me for my lifetime, just as the appalling shock of the explosion of the space-shuttle *Challenger* still haunts me.

In Rome, and, I believe, all round the world, wherever there are men and women of goodwill, the mass prayers for the healing of Pope John Paul II were continuous, day and night, and the miracle of that kindly, elderly man's recovery is self-evident.

I cannot accept the flip explanation that this was just coincidence, because I have seen too much evidence, during the course of my life, that indicates the contrary.

I am certain that those massed, *positive* prayers helped His Holiness to a full and miraculous recovery. This same belief is held by many millions of others, and I am not a Catholic, though all my Peruvian family are members of that faith.

As one who served with the Poles for some months during the war, I long have been an admirer of these deeply mystical people, and I can understand the fervent loyalty that such a man as Pope John Paul II inspires. I can see why so much power was generated by his world congregations, and by millions of others, in their massed positive prayers.

Therefore, I believe that his recovery was miraculous!

How then do healers and their positive energies work?

Not being a qualified physician, I have had to go to my medical friends, to get a valid picture of the workings of the human body.

Open-minded medical practitioners, like Doctor Stanley Rose, a very experienced physician and psychiatrist in Birmingham, and Doctor Michael Dixon, our family physician, in Surrey, among many others, have discussed healing with me, many times.

All of them seemed to be in general agreement, that a positive attitude towards recovery on the part of the patient, and a sympathetic and outgoing approach by the attending physician to the patient, who is suffering from any severe condition or critical illness, is the first essential in establishing a good healing rapport.

Secondly, all these experienced doctors have a deep and enduring faith in the power of positive thinking, and combine their unquestioned skill in the practice of their art, with their own caring humanity.

Yet, somehow they are able to distance themselves sufficiently from too close an identification with their patients, to be able to survive in a good state of health, under the extraordinary stress that the practice of medicine imposes on sensitive physicians.

From what they have told me, it would appear that the vital clues to the whole self-healing process lie in the nervous system, which, through the brain and, therefore, the mind, of the patient, control all the voluntary and involuntary functions of the body. This applies as much to the respiratory and circulatory systems, as to the glandular and immunization systems and to all the other complex mechanisms which sustain life in the miracle that we call the human body.

Basically, the electro-chemical process, without which life, as we know it, cannot exist, is the key to the whole question of how healing can take place.

Recently, at the Maimonedes Centre in New York, orthopaedic surgeons and physicians carried out a series of remarkable experiments, aimed at accelerating the healing process in traumatized osteo-tissue (fractured bones). Sterilized electrodes were inserted into either end of the fractured bones, through the medullary channels (along which the appropriate nerves run, like wires through electrical ducting). A weak electric current, at a very low amperage, was passed continually through the electrodes, thereby generating a weak electro-magnetic field, in the area of the traumatized osteo-tissue.

I understand that the patients experienced nothing more than a slight tingling sensation, but the regeneration of the fractured bone tissues was accelerated by a very significant amount. (I have been told that this was of the order of 200–300 per cent *above* the normal rate of healing.)

Experiments that also merit close examination, in trying to understand the processes involved in healing, in the whollistic sense, were conducted by two Russian physicists, Doctors Valery and Semenyov Kirlian, in the university laboratory in Khasakstan.

These experiments consisted of passing high-voltage, high-frequency, electric currents through themselves and other volunteers, while photographs were taken of the emission of these electrical charges through their fingers. This was done by placing their hands on photographic plates, enclosed in a light-tight box.

When the film was developed, it clearly showed an impressive aura surrounding each finger, as a point of discharge of the high-frequency electrical charge.

In the case of a number of genuine healers, who also were the subject of these experiments, the extent of these auras, from an identical charge of electric current, of the same high frequency and voltage, showed a marked *increase* in the size of the resultant discharge of these energies, through the fingertips.

Furthermore, in additional experiments, carried out by the same Russian team, using various substances, both organic and inorganic, ranging from plant leaves, and flowers, to mineral crystals, the photographically recorded results exactly matched the observed results, as described and drawn by a number of sensitives, who had been the subject of a series of experiments carried out in Germany, during the last century.

These earlier experiments had been conducted by a successful German industrial-chemist, Baron Von Reichenbach, the discoverer of creosote and the inventor of the process for the industrial production of paraffin.

Baron Von Reichenbach's fascinating book *Letters on Od and Magnetism* describing his experiments with 'Odic' force, as he named it, after Odin, the ancient Nordic

153

God, brought down on him the scorn and ridicule of the Berlin Academy of Science, from which he was asked to resign.

This extraordinary book, published in the last century, and translated into English, from Von Reichenbach's original work, by Doctor William Gregory, a Scottish chemist, also contained a series of engravings in the appendix. These *exactly matched* the later photographic evidence, produced by the Kirlians, and recently duplicated by two Birmingham physicists, who published their results in their book *The Loom of Creation*.

What Von Reichenbach did, in the last century, and for which he was scientifically martyred by the Establishment of his time, was to use the talents of over a hundred sensitives of his acquaintance for a series of experiments. These were held in complete darkness, to ascertain whether these subjects could see and describe the emanations of subtle (Odic) force, from crystals, plants, leaves and similar substances, just as the Kirlians did a hundred years later, and which Von Reichenbach believed was generated by both organic and inorganic matter.

The engravings in the Baron's translated work, showed the result of these experiments which were carried out over a twenty-year period. Their accompanying notes, regarding the colour and apparent size and shape of the observed emanations of Odic force, show, as already mentioned, that these nineteenth-century engravings exactly *duplicated* the twentieth-century experiments, by both the Russian and British physicists.

Like Galileo, and Nikola Tesla, the unfortunate Baron Von Reichenbach, an equally respected scientist, was derided and wiped out, temporarily, from scientific history and contemporary textbooks by the technological Establishments of their respective eras.

To return to healing, it seems to me that healers have the ability to draw upon the ambient energy in the atmosphere which we breathe, and which is generated by the presence of super-abundant free electrons within the ionospheric vault.

I also believe that genuine healers have a certain physical make-up which in some way is subtly different to other bodies, in that they may well possess some form of genetic modification to their systems, in terms of the nerves and glandular structure of the body, making them capable of transforming this raw energy into another form, which, for convenience, I shall refer to as: 'Life Force'.

This manifests itself as the marked physical vitality that genuine healers, whom I have known and with whom I have worked, seem to possess, in abundance.

I believe that it is this same 'Life Force', which is also perhaps the 'Odic' force of Von Reichenbach's theories, that is the source of the healing energies that seem to flow from the healer to the debilitated recipient, who, presumably, is badly in need of such vitality.

I do not regard this theory as being too fanciful for consideration, and neither do a number of my medically, and scientifically, qualified friends.

Nevertheless, I offer it only as a *possible* solution to the question of where the healer gets his, or her, healing energies. Could this 'Life Force', 'Odic' energy, or whatever you like to call it, also be the source of the demonstrably effective power of *massed* prayer, i.e. positive energy, which so evidently helped the British people and their Allies, to resist the might of the Nazi war machine?

I find that to be a distinct possibility, for the power of positive thinking certainly seems to be an effective weapon against terrorism, such as that generated by the Nazis, or other kinds of evil, and, presumably, works against all destructive forces, such as disease, in whatever form it attacks us. Remove the fear and you effectively reduce the power of evil in proportion, and the same applies to most diseases, for stress is a vital factor in all illnesses.

I believe that genuine, whollistic healing is vitally important to the well-being of a patient, who is suffering from any form of severely debilitating disease, or chronic condition. Furthermore, I believe that the term patient can be extended to refer to a community, to a nation, or, for that matter, to all humanity, or even to the entire living entity of the planet, itself.

In the case of whollistic healing, I strongly object to this being referred to as: 'Alternative Medicine', because this implies the rejection of *all* conventional healing methods, used in the practice of the great arts of medicine and surgery, which are the products of many centuries of research, development and practice, by hundreds of thousands of dedicated men and women. I prefer to use the term: 'Complementary' healing, i.e. as an adjunct to conventional medicine and surgery.

Why should I be so interested in healing?

Twice in my lifetime I have been helped, enormously, by healers.

The first occasion was in 1942, when a short time after I had finally been accepted for aircrew training by the Royal Air Force, I was given, along with two other cadets, an untreated combined 'serum', which, actually, contained the *cultures* of typhus, typhoid and tetanus.

This normally safe combined injection was administered, routinely, to all aircrew going overseas for their final flying training. In the case of the three of us, something had gone wrong with the preparation of these inoculations. We were the last three cadets, on the end of a long line of trainee aircrew and I had noticed the medical orderly change the bottle, which he had been using to refill the large hypodermic syringe, with which we were being inoculated.

Within hours, one cadet was dead, another lay paralysed and I was in agony, bent like a bow, in the course of severe and agonizing convulsions.

Mercifully, I remember little of what followed, as the RAF doctors and nurses, at the Central Sick Quarters, fought for my life, nearly losing me several times in the process. When I finally returned to my body, from an extraordinary experience of mental projection into what seemed to be another, awe-inspiring dimension of shining light and contrasting velvet darkness, I lay, between life and death, for another day, drifting off into unconsciousness, between bouts of extreme pain.

It took six months and the efforts of two healers, one of whom was my father, to restore me to a semblance of physical fitness.

The RAF wanted to discharge me, with a pension, but I managed to persuade the authorities to retain my services, and, as membership of the aircrew was now denied me, my eyesight having suffered severely in the process, I was offered a commission in Intelligence.

The second time that I nearly passed, permanently, out of my body, was in 1960, when, following a severe bout of double pneumonia, I developed pulmonary emboli (blood clots in the lungs). Had it not been for the quick-wittedness of a young Lebanese nurse, who instantly recognized the symptoms of the embolism, which originated agonizingly in my groin, I would not be writing these words.

Yet again a grim battle for my life was fought and won.

Once more, a healer, this time my father's housekeeper, Florrie Dott, a splendid Northumbrian lady, helped me to regain my health.

But for her massive transference of vital energy, I would have lost my left leg from widespread gangrene, a condition which I recognized, with horror, from my wartime experiences with the badly-wounded friends I had visited in hospital.

The smell of gas-gangrene is unforgettable!

In my case, the specialist, Doctor Barry Murray, was going to amputate the limb, but I begged him to hold off for twenty-four hours. Reluctantly, he agreed, but insisted that this must be the deadline. If there was no improvement, the gangrenous limb would have to be removed, or I would die.

Meanwhile, the cheerful, middle-aged housekeeper, who had kept Pop alive and comfortable for years, and who was endowed with great energy and physical strength, visited me in Bolingbroke Hospital, and gave me an hour of uninterrupted healing. Within minutes, I had drifted off into a blissfully painless sleep and, once again I left my body, to enter that same dimension of light and soft, warm darkness, that I remembered so vividly from my dying experience, in 1942.

When I returned to my body, I felt relaxed and free from pain, and, during the course of the night, my left leg changed from the nauseating, swollen condition of gangrenous flesh and tissue, to a more normal and much healthier appearance.

What was more, that awful smell of gangrene had gone!

Doctor Murray arrived early, ready to perform the amputation, and could hardly believe the radical change in my condition.

I told him, frankly, what had happened and he was open-minded enough not to scoff at the possibility of a 'miraculous' healing. (His own words.) In fact, he told me that he had seen one or two previous cases of the same sort of remarkable remission in severely-ill patients, following treatment by a healer.

It took me six months to walk again, but I then was able to write and perform in my successful *It's a Square World* series, which ran for over four years as a top comedy show on the BBC, eventually winning the Grand Prix de la Presse, at Montreux, the *first* BBC comedy show ever to do so.

Lastly, I should like to tell you about the role that healing can play, in helping to allay the agonies of grief, that most people suffer, following the loss of someone they love.

Having known, along with my family, the pain of such grief for the loss of our three splendid children, as adults, and the recent passing of our much-loved 'Nursie', who was our loyal and wonderful friend for over thirty-six years, I can vouch for the help that positive thinking has given to me.

It also has helped my surviving son and daughter to come to terms with their own sorrow, and I hope that my wife, Clementina, now feels less of that gut-wrenching agony that grief brings in its wake. Inevitably, it is a more terrible experience for the mother, who has carried the child during pregnancy, to accept the loss of the physical presence of her children, when they die.

I can only strongly recommend the healing effect of positive thinking, in learning to cope with that loss.

The feelings of guilt, usually totally undeserved, that tend to haunt the living when someone they love is killed in a car, motor-cycle, plane or other type of violent accident, or dies through sudden illness, should be nullified as quickly as possible, if their own health is not to suffer.

Those torturing thoughts that, somehow, no matter how far-fetched, the grieving relation, lover or close friend might have been instrumental in preventing the accident, must be discarded because they are only the product of shock and negative thinking.

The sooner the person who is grieving can accept the situation and understand that in *no* way can their sense of sorrow and helplessness to rectify the tragic circumstances do anything constructive for the rest of the sorrowing family, or help to ease their own pain, the sooner they themselves will be able to return to normality and get on with the important business of living.

Obviously, in the case of a long illness preceding death, as opposed to a sudden fatality, the situation itself often presents a partial solution to the problem of extended grief, if the surviving members of the family consider the alternative, of an even longer period of suffering on the part of the deceased, and realize how much more merciful the passing had been under the circumstances.

Coping with grief is not just a question of semantics, or blind faith, for there is no immediate solution to that terrible sense of physical loss and shock, that is felt by so many people every day. Because of this, it has always seemed to me that the natural way in which animals deal with that same numbing shock is the best way for humans to behave, as well.

The howling cries of the mate, or cubs, which can rend the heart of even hardened hunters, is the quickest and best way for that animal to get rid of the temporary paralysis of grief, which often can lead to its own destruction.

This is Nature's own way of dealing with the problem, and, like all natural things, it is the best. Therefore, howl your heart out and then fall into the exhausted sleep that usually succeeds that release of all the pent-up emotion inside you.

If you are trying to comfort someone who is weeping and shrieking hysterically, the worst thing you can do is to stop them by slapping them. That sort of drastic treatment may be unavoidable, if you are trying to drag the grieving person away from a source of imminent danger, like a fire, a possible explosion, a flood, a sinking vessel or some such disaster.

I believe, and I am not alone in this, that arresting the natural process of hysterical grief, while the person is getting rid of the effects of shock, can be a very harmful thing. This is where a genuine healer can be of such benefit and help to a sorrowing person; by helping to replenish the vitality, which is being drained from the sufferer, further weakening the bereaved person and lowering their powers of resistance, in a vicious circle of more grief, less strength, and, consequently, less ability to control their emotions.

Once again, it is all a question of commonsense, and knowing how far to go to comfort the bereaved, without over-indulging their sense of self-pity, which can also be the motivating force behind the display of grief.

Try to think positively! That is a piece of advice which I know, from bitter experience in this area of human behaviour, is far easier to give, than to adopt. It is however, the most sensible course of action to take!

This is always the case, except in dire emergencies, where sleep itself is the best healer and the sufferer will often wake feeling stronger and more able to cope with the numbing sense of physical loss, that is natural in these tragic circumstance.

Deep religious faith also can be of immeasurable help, but that, in itself, is another manifestation of positive thinking.

The best advice I can give, is to get on with comforting others, who may be suffering as much or even more than you are. That positive act of love is also a great self-healing force, for the ones who make that supreme effort.

Healing and self-healing are all part of natural law, and the further we depart from Nature, the more difficult we make our lives.

CHAPTER EIGHT

Psychic attack

Is such a thing as a psychic attack possible?

Judging by my experiences, I say: 'Yes. Very much so!'

Furthermore, these psychic attacks are far more widespread than people realize.

Let us start by defining the words.

Psychic means: appertaining to the psyche, which is defined as the soul, or mind.

Therefore, we are using these words to describe an attack on the mind, or the soul, if you believe such an entity exists.

Propaganda, that dark art of twisting the truth to suit the circumstance, is essentially a form of psychic attack. It was first practised on a global scale during the First World War. It achieved even greater importance with the introduction of radio, both before and during the Second World War and now has become an integral and inescapable part of our lives with the arrival of television in our living-rooms.

From those crude early beginnings, in 1914, when British newspapers, like the ultra-chauvinist *John Bull*, carried banner headlines such as: 'Boche Bayonets Belgian Babies' and other dreadful rubbish, the use of Propaganda has grown into the perverted art which daily affects our lives.

By 1918, American newspapers raged: 'American troops charge over the top, with the cry of "*Lusitania*" on their lips'.

162

This, supposedly, was as a direct result of the loss to a German U-boat torpedo of the British liner *Lusitania*, which with many Americans aboard was sunk off the south coast of Ireland in 1915, thereby theoretically precipitating the American participation in the war by 1917.

Actually, it already had been decided by America in secret agreement with the Allied governments, that the time had come for the United States to join in the world conflict, although because of her avowed intention of keeping out of European power politics, America had managed to preserve her neutrality for nearly three years.

Nevertheless, President Wilson was finally forced into informing Congress that Germany was planning a military coup against the United States, as well as being about to wage unrestricted submarine warfare against *all* neutral shipping.

The plan, devised by General Ludendorff of the German General Staff, envisaged a massive raid on the southwestern American states of New Mexico and California by *Mexican* forces, secretly reinforced by German officers and NCOs and armed with German machine guns and artillery.

Ludendorff was interested in the occult and was, reputedly, a member of the notorious 'OTO' (*Ordo Templi Orientis*), a German magical society founded by Theodore Reuss, a notorious Teutonic ritual-magician. This secret society was associated with the British 'Order of the Golden Dawn', and had originally authorized that ritual group's formation, a tact that interested British Intelligence. In essence this Mexican plot was very like the same German general's 'Sealed Train' operation, which secretly sent Lenin by rail into Russia, armed with guns, gold, and a tough band of revolutionaries. This clandestine plan had culminated in the 'October Revolution', and effectively put an end to the Tzarist monarchy and Imperial Russia's part in the First World War.

For the similar covert operation against Mexico, Ludendorff had convinced the Kaiser to allow the use of large ocean-going U-boats, as the equivalent of the 'Sealed Train', to carry these vital supplies to the Mexican dissidents. He had also concocted a similar subversive plan aimed at the overthrow of the Japanese government.

The Mexican conspiracy had only come to light, due to the interception by British Naval Intelligence of a cable sent to the German ambassador in Mexico by a top German Foreign Office functionary, called Zimmerman.

It was in cypher but British Naval Intelligence already possessed a copy of the Imperial German Navy's Code, which had been passed on to them by a Russian Naval Intelligence officer, when the German cruiser *Magdeberg* had been destroyed by the Russians in the Baltic within days of the start of the war.

Once the United States Congress heard of this conspiracy – which became known as the 'Zimmerman Telegram' – there was no alternative for America but to declare war on Germany.

To me, this other Ludendorff Conspiracy, is a prime example of a psychic attack as well as a physical one on a grand scale, i.e. a clandestine effort to harm an enemy or rival, *without* their knowledge.

Since those days the global-ranging radio and television networks of the major powers operate a continuous psychological bombardment of subtle, and not so subtle, propaganda against their rivals, in a world struggle for power.

Both sides disseminate, via satellites, their 'disinformation' services of politically-angled propaganda to the whole world. It has become a very large and expensive industry, in which every shade of political opinion, from extreme right to extreme left, as well as powerful commercial interests attempt to win the advantage in this continual battle for the mind.

This constitutes, in my opinion, a continual psychic or psychological attack aimed at the mind of the people.

For example, modern Soviet Russia produces and sells to countries like Britain excellent radios with a world-wide range. These are equipped with special sets of crystals tuned to receive the super-powerful transmitters of the Communist global blanket of propaganda in all languages; a neat professional achievement in the art of disinformation.

I recently saw an advertisement, (I believe it was in *The Times*) for these radio sets, selling for less than £35, for instruments that must cost well over that price to manufacture.

When any nation is taken over by a military coup, the first objective is to move in and capture the radio and television stations, from which 'high-ground', the new regime can consolidate and control the coup.

It is a well-known fact that the 'Schwarze Kapelle', the German generals' bomb-plot to overthrow Hitler by assassination in 1944, failed largely due to the generals' oversight in not capturing and operating the entire German radio network, which immediately gave the lie to their claim that the Führer was dead.

Presumably profiting by this lesson, the Marxist military junta which took over Peru, in 1969, sent in its 'task force' with the cleaners, first thing in the morning, thereby seizing control of all the radio and television network stations, especially in the capital city of Lima, by 6 a.m. When the citizens of Lima and other major Peruvian cities switched on their radios or television sets at breakfast time there, as usual, were the familiar voices and faces of their announcers and newscasters, wishing them *'Buenas Dias'*.

The only difference was that they were reading news bulletins which were being issued from the headquarters of the new revolutionary military government.

By the time the people were on their way to work, every important centre of government and seat of power, the airports, harbours, railway and bus stations, post offices, electricity and gas plants, town halls, hospitals and employment offices were all under revolutionary military guard.

Nobody could do anything because the nerve-centre, i.e. the transmitters of information, had been taken over as the prime target.

In our present civilization, no matter where a centre of population is located, the main and constant battle is for the mind. Therefore, I believe that we are all under constant psychic attack of one kind or another.

That is why I am convinced that it is vitally important for everyone to open his or her mind to realize the extent of the propaganda, both commercial and political, that continually bombards every one of us, including our children, who are being attacked just as heavily as we are.

If you think this is a wild statement, remember that it is being made by someone who has spent the past forty-two years of his life involved in the media in all its forms, and who during the last war served for nearly three years in RAF Intelligence. So, at least, I know and understand the nature and methodology of propaganda, and the effective use of disinformation.

I know how it is done and I can assess, within reason, to what extent the information being transmitted is politically, or commercially influenced, according to the sources from which it emanates.

If you still find these statements hard to believe, consider an average day in the life of an ordinary family, pretty well anywhere in the world.

At daybreak, the first action on waking is for some member of the family to switch on the radio or television, or both, to catch the weather-forecast and to listen to the day's news, sport and travel information.

The morning paper is then read and throughout the day, until the working members of the household return from the factory, office, store, or institution where they are employed, news bulletins are listened to and often discussed.

On their return home with the children, if any, the TV is soon switched on and usually watched until the family retires to bed.

Quite apart from the endless commercial propaganda that assails us we are seldom free from the insidious influence of the media, and many a good night's sleep has been sabotaged by some particularly grisly late-night bulletin, dwelling on the over-dramatized aspects of some crisis in the country's affairs. Most recently we experienced this in Britain during the Falklands conflict.

All this, usually, is presented by familiar television and radio personalities, and one of the subtle inferences of propaganda disseminated by these means is that comforting familiarity imparts a sense of validity to whatever these popular personalities are saying or *reading*.

It would never occur to the listener, or viewer, that these familiar voices and smiling faces would ever lie to them, consciously or unconsciously.

Equally, it seldom occurs to the radio or television announcers *themselves*, that what they are reading from the script or teleprompter in front of them could be untrue because it issues from their own programme editors and scriptwriters.

It would be like journalists doubting Reuters or Press Association releases, in the days when newspapers were the main organs of propaganda. I know that, because for a few months during 1940, I worked with a famous photographic news agency, Keystone Press, and I believed everything that the wartime Ministry of Information handed to us.

The slant put on the news depends on whoever has been appointed to run the network, or on those, at the middle-management and editorial level, who control the flow of information, through the department of news and current affairs.

You would be amazed how easy it is for a television or radio scriptwriter, consciously or unconsciously, to subtly angle the thrust of a news story, let alone the difference that can be made to a newscast, by the presenter emphasizing certain key words in the script.

This may be done *unconsciously* by a newsreader, who is particularly in sympathy with the angling of a news item, understandably in the case of the plight of starving people, especially children.

However, such angling and emphasis on certain 'buzz-words', as they are called, in items of a political nature where the bias of the writer and that of the presenter are both in alignment, can lead to a false interpretation of the news item, thereby conveying a rather different version of the facts to the listener or viewer, who usually accepts the news at its face value.

These 'buzz-words' tend to evoke mental images, usually of an extreme political nature, such as: Fascist, Neo-Nazi, Chauvinist, Imperialist, Racist, Capitalist etc., or conversely: Terrorist, Political Assassin, Red Menace, Anarchist, Trotskyite, *et al*.

This is why it is vitally important for the true freedom of the Press to be maintained and censorship, even in a situation like the Falklands conflict, to be kept to the minimum, but such censorship must *also* be understood to apply to the *conscious* angling of news and current affairs in radio and television programmes, for personal or political motives, within the structure of the networks themselves.

Naturally, this ideal cannot apply anywhere but in a democracy, because, in totalitarian countries, all news and current affairs are directly under the control of the Ministry of Propaganda, and therefore only reflect the power politics of the current regime, be they right-wing or left-wing inclined.

In a democracy this hard-won and cherished freedom must not be interpreted as a licence to make any statement, no matter how far removed from the truth it may be, in order to sensationalize the news item or programme, in an unscrupulous attempt to increase newspaper circulation, or television and radio viewing and listening figures, whether for commercial or political reasons.

It is indeed a very narrow path to tread and one which is fraught with difficulties and it entirely depends on the self-discipline of the teams of journalists, scriptwriters, editors and presenters, engaged on the very responsible task of news-gathering and its impartial presentation. It is undoubtedly one of the most responsible jobs in the world.

But, in the end, the truth pays off in the confidence of the public in their Press and, most important, in the media of radio and television journalism, where the effect on the viewer and listener is more immediate and when they cannot re-examine the bulletins at leisure, without recording them.

One of the December 1987 issues of the American *TV Guide*, which is one of the most widely-read weekly pocket magazines in the world, carried an article with a most disturbing indictment of many of America's top news programmes.

It virtually accused several of the top US newscasters of many instances of careless inaccuracy, followed by subsequent lack of interest and tardiness on the part of the network in apologizing to the injured parties concerned.

It went on to condemn the practice of blatant newscasting inaccuracies as being wholly unacceptable in the present state of the art, with immediate global satellite coverage of all sources of the news media.

During the Falklands crisis, the BBC seemed to suffer somewhat from this type of news coverage, though it had some excuse in being hampered by the clumsy bulletins issued by the British Ministry of Defence. However, that does not explain or justify the general air of doom and gloom with which new, young and unfamiliar television newscasters relayed the latest coverage of that grim struggle.

Surely, at such a time of national and international crisis familiar newscasters would have been far more reassuring to the worried British public, but, abruptly, these new men and women appeared on our screens and somewhat ineptly, for they were then evidently inexperienced in the art of television presentation, read the news bulletins which were anything but encouraging.

During the last war, BBC newsreaders like Bruce Belfrage, Alvar Liddell and their chief, John Snagge, always personally identified themselves before broadcasting these bulletins, saying, for instance: 'Here is the nine o'clock news, and this is Bruce Belfrage reading it.'

Furthermore, to any experienced professional television performer, it became evident that these new broadcasters, by their very attitudes and tone of voice, were resentful of Prime Minister Margaret Thatcher's decision to attack the invading Argentine forces. Moreover, judging by some of the content of these bulletins and by the way that they were being read, an apparent bias, seemingly in favour of the Argentinians, became disturbingly apparent.

I pointed this out to a BBC official, and reminded him that the repressive Argentine military junta was the most evil organization since the Nazis, and was itself responsible for the disappearance and secret murder of over twelve thousand dissidents. I told him that anyone who fought such a repellent entity was on the side of the Angels.

Being half South-American and a British ex-serviceman myself, I felt a great sympathy for *all* the youngsters involved in battle, on *both* sides of this needless conflict, which should have been solved politically, years before. Therefore, I could hardly remain silent in the face of this extraordinary broadcasting attitude, which was so different to that of the BBC, during the Second World War.

I certainly do not remember any such bias becoming evident in favour of the Nazis, in those days. Yet during the actual conflict we had British television interviewers in Argentina talking to sympathizers with that appalling regime. The Argentine government certainly would not have allowed dissidents to voice their opinions.

To many professional ex-broadcasters, like the late Alvar Liddell who had been one of the top BBC newsreaders, the whole situation regarding the reportage of the Falklands crisis was so appalling that he spoke out against these practices. This normally quiet and restrained man, whose work was regarded as an example of the highest criterion in unbiased newscasting was, atypically, upset and he protested publicly and vehemently against the way the media was handling the news.

He was particularly disturbed by the emphasis, consciously or unconsciously, being used by newsreaders, for in his day when the BBC's reputation for impartiality and accuracy in broadcasting was being made world famous, such melodramatization of a news bulletin was specifically forbidden. The standing instruction for newsreaders was to report the facts as known and *without emotion*. As you can imagine this was difficult to do in wartime, but it had been carried out with extraordinary skill, even when a bomb hit Broadcasting House while the news was being read by Bruce Belfrage, who scarcely faltered.

For inexperienced newsreaders to do this is extremely difficult.

Commercial broadcasting networks within a democracy are usually bound by rigid codes of practice in advertising and they soon feel the weight of authority if they flagrantly digress from the strict guide-lines, which are part of the conditions of their broadcasting licence.

But, for years, the BBC has had far more flexibility, especially during the nine-year reign of the late Sir Hugh Carleton Greene as Director General, when many of the former strict BBC directives which had been issued by the Calvinistic Scot, Sir John Reith, a former DG, were scrapped.

Instead, Sir Hugh gave free rein to anyone whose radical thinking could make a dent in the old, treasured image of 'Auntie Beeb'. These licensees of Greene's new regime were *invariably* radically left-wing in their political thinking.

One cannot just ignore that complete revolution in the British Broadcasting Corporation and pretend that it didn't happen. It did! And the present state of broadcasting in Britain today, which has gone a long way down the road of permissiveness, is the poorer because of it.

Moreover, the BBC's international influence affected broadcasting standards throughout the English-speaking democracies, worldwide.

Following the Corporation's new permissive attitude to broadcasting, Canada, Australia, New Zealand and even the United States, which was rigidly controlled by many moral conventions but admired the BBC, lowered their standards accordingly. Furthermore, any attempt to return to the old tenets of good taste and impartiality were greeted with loud cries of 'reactionary censorship!'

The revolution, often in the form of such psychological attacks on selected political personalities, many of them international, was well on its way.

If you doubt the validity of these statements ask yourselves if the British media's account of Watergate and the savage persecution of Richard Nixon would have been quite so self-righteous, had he been a left-wing, rather than a right-wing president.

Furthermore, if you consider the outstanding differences between the pre-1964 content of BBC programmes and today's 'almost anything goes' attitude of the Corporation to radio and television broadcasting, you will be more than surprised. Yet the BBC still rides high, globally, on the strength of its previous record for fair reporting and integrity, which was the result of the dedicated hard work of so many good men and women, some of whom I had been lucky enough to work with.

Therefore, my respect and affection for the actual professionals who keep the BBC going as a world-leader in broadcasting technology is as high as ever. By this, of course, I mean the many skilled engineers and dedicated artists, and all the true craftsmen and craftswomen involved in the professional broadcasting structure of the BBC, many of whom I have long counted as friends and valued colleagues.

It is only towards part of the Directorate and middle-management structure of the BBC *at those particular times*, that any of these valid criticisms are directed, and once again there is plenty of evidence to back up these statements.

I first became associated with the BBC, in 1946, but I was never a staff member, though I was offered a job several times, prior to 1963. As already mentioned, I have been active in broadcasting in both radio and television as a freelance performer and scriptwriter for over forty-two years.

I understand from a recent letter to me from the assistant head of the BBC's legal department that only *one* programme of my top-rated comedy series (*It's a Square World*) has been kept in BBC Archives. This loss includes the programme that won the *first ever* television comedy award to the BBC, at Montreux (The Grand Prix de La Presse), in 1963. However, I still hope that this information may prove to be incorrect, and I am pursuing at present this line of enquiry.

To accept that all those years of hard work have been wiped out is a bitter pill for any professional to swallow. Moreover, none of my fifty-one *Goon Show* radio programmes, of which I was a founder member and one of the original cast, and to which I contributed many of the comedy ideas and concepts, have been retained by the BBC, nor have any of these early *Goon Shows*, in which I participated, ever been repeated.

I understand that the first show which was repeated was the one *after* I left. Surely this is rather too much of a coincidence.

But according to information from the BBC's legal department, over fifty shows of *It's a Square World*,

173

recorded and transmitted between 1960 and the end of 1964 and from which so many first-class performers, like Dick Emery, Clive Dunn, Frank Thornton, and Ronnie Barker emerged as first-class performers, apparently have been wiped from television history (apart from one example from the 1961 series), and no explanation, restitution or apology has been made to me.

In view of the fact that BBC contracts *specifically* demand the right to retain and broadcast extracts from *all* the shows that they make: '. . . in programmes of a reminiscent or historical nature. . . .' and that the *Monty Python* shows and *The Two Ronnies* among many others, have been kept in their entirety, it seems strange that practically *all* my *Square World* shows were deliberately wiped. Especially as they have been described in the Press, by top television critic Philip Purser, as being: '. . . one of the seminal sources, if not *the* seminal source . . . from which many subsequent TV comedy series drew their inspiration.. . .'

In 1963 I had *unconsciously* offended Sir Hugh Carleton Greene, by refusing to angle, politically, my programmes in the form of satire to be directed *solely* against the Macmillan, i.e. Conservative government.

This approach had been made to me by an important official of the BBC, on behalf of the DG, but I rejected it, in view of the licence fee having to be paid by *all* members of the public with a radio or television set, *no matter what their political persuasions might be.*

I said that I would be delighted to 'send-up' *every* political party, *equally*, but that I couldn't zero in on just one of them. That would have been a betrayal of every principle, for which so many of my wartime comrades had laid down their lives.

Old-fashioned as this attitude may seem to be, in this present pragmatic world, that is how I felt at the time, and it is still the way I feel today.

Certainly that decision of mine seemed to have terminated my television career with the BBC, at its peak, for *Square World* by then had a very large public viewing figure.

During the General Election of the following year, one of my television programmes, innocently made about the sinking of the Houses of Parliament, by cannon-fire from a Chinese junk, was cancelled, as it accidentally coincided with the election, a contingency I could not possibly have guessed would happen. Almost immediately, a personal attack was made against me by Sir Hugh, as Director General of the BBC, in the *Sunday Telegraph*, claiming that he had *seen* the programme and cancelled it because of its deliberately malicious contents.

I protested, with proof that Carleton Greene had misled the *Sunday Telegraph* readers, in that he could not possibly have *seen* the programme, which was still in many unedited pieces, and therefore a copy could not have been shown to him, in the manner he so minutely described.

As a result I received a vague sort of apology couched in odd terms. This was signed by his assistant, Kenneth Adam, and no mention *whatsoever* was made of Carleton Greene's name!

I remembered that Sir Hugh had been a leading member of MI6, during the war, and had worked at the secret headquarters, at Bletchley Park, creating antifascist propaganda, with Sefton Delmer and Richard Crossman, in an organization which was aptly nicknamed: 'The Ministry of Disinformation'.

But why his continued anonymity was being preserved by his assistant, in this odd letter, I have no idea.

The BBC, under Greene's radical, determined and ruthless direction, soon changed its former 'Auntie Beeb' image into one of almost total permissiveness, in support of the image of the new permissive society, to a degree that provoked widespread public protest, which Sir Hugh completely ignored.

In effect, the Corporation became, demonstrably, hostile to most of the old, accepted standards of behaviour.

I often wonder what motives prompted this powerfully placed man to carry out these radical changes, in the vitally important media of British television and radio broadcasting, which could and in fact did have such a widespread global effect, by carrying the message of permissiveness around the world.

If you doubt that, compare the standards of today's television and radio broadcasting, world-wide, *except in totalitarian countries*, with those immediately prior to Carleton Greene's nine-year regime at the BBC.

I think you will be surprised at the result!

It may be purely coincidental that Sir Hugh, who had remained a close friend of Kim Philby after the latter's defection to the Soviet Union, frequently visited Russia and that, subsequently, he has been described by the Russians as: 'The best Director General the BBC ever had,' this extraordinary statement having been made in a leading Moscow newspaper.

Incidentally, I was told by an official at the 1963 Montreux festival, that I also would have won the coveted Golden Rose award, as well as the Grand Press prize, had *It's a Square World*, *not* included a gentle send-up of the United Nations, with Kruschev beating the podium in time to the playing of *Black Eyes*, the famous old Russian song. This was, supposedly, as a member of a *Juke Box Jury* into which I had, with the aid of my clever film editor, converted the UN Assembly.

This unusual item was greeted with loud laughter and applause by the international delegates to the Montreux TV festival, but apparently offended the Russian judge, who for the *first time ever*, surprisingly and at the last minute, had been included on the international panel.

His official protest cost me the Golden Rose, and further widened the gap between Carleton Greene, who was furious, and myself.

My position with the BBC soon became untenable and, after I left, my television appearances with the Corporation, apart from one short series of children's programmes, many years later *after* Carleton Greene had been superseded, were only desultory and infrequent.

I also suddenly found myself *persona non grata* with BBC radio.

In fact, it was just as though I had been 'blacklisted', something that is next to impossible to prove, but which is indicated by the undeniable circumstantial evidence of no work being offered me by the Corporation for many years.

That to me is yet another piece of evidence for the existence of a psychic, or psychological, attack.

I have included these disturbing facts to emphasize the power afforded to the heads of these great networks of propaganda and mind-manipulation. For, when they are misused, they can cause untold damage.

I know from bitter experience how they can affect the lives and careers of hard-working professional writers and performers, and an outstanding example of *right-wing* action of this kind is frequently cited by the media, under the title of *The Hollywood Ten*, referring to the savage persecution of ten well-known left-wing writers and performers in the United States, during the poisonous McCarthy era. I am certainly not the first, nor will I be the last, to suffer at the hands of such vindictive manipulators of power.

'Surely, you don't believe in the conspiracy theory?'

I can almost hear that question being asked.

My answer is always the same.

'To which of the world's numerous pragmatic conspiracies are you referring?'

After all there are so many, ranging from the Mafia, through the Union Corse, the Chinese Triads, certain international cartels, some global banking, most arms dealers, a number of huge industrial conglomerates, narcotics smuggling-rings and the like, to the alleged clandestine conspiracy within the Vatican itself (the infamous P2 Lodge).

177

These are actual conspiracies, most of which wield enormous power in their spheres of influence, some of them on an international scale.

They are in stark contrast to those hoary old red-herrings, the supposed 'Protocols of the Elders of Zion', the equally spurious 'World Threat of Freemasonry', and the alleged 'Great Catholic Conspiracy'.

These so-called menaces to the peace of the world are of the 'Fu-Manchu' variety of purple fiction presented as fact, involving Liberal Jews, well-meaning Freemasons and dedicated Roman Catholic priests and nuns. They are all outstanding demonstrations of the power of deliberate psychic attacks, and are believed in by many people.

A virulent psychological attack made on the public and private reputation of an individual, was apparent in the sensational Profumo case, which had brought about the 1964 election and the consequent defeat of the Tory party, under Harold Macmillan.

This dramatic public scandal involved a young man called Stephen Ward, described by the media as a social-ite osteopath and physiotherapist. I had known him quite well, and found him to be a charming conversationalist. He had skilfully treated minor injuries sustained by many of my friends during theatrical performances, and he was professionally *persona grata* in London's West End theatres.

Moreover, I had often discussed aspects of the para-normal with him, for he had an intense interest in the occult, as Stephen Ward referred to the subject of our conversations.

He also implied that he was an avowed Marxist, despite his socialite ambitions, so his involvement with a Captain Ivanov of the KGB had come to me as no surprise.

But I had not realized how deeply Ward was involved with the paranormal, until he invited me to join his circle. Apparently, this strange group was based on an eighteenth-century cover of hell-raisers, who had called themselves 'The Hell-Fire Club'.

This previous coven of ritual-magicians had been situated at High Wycombe, nearly two centuries before, and had been led, for some thirty-seven years, by Sir Francis Dashwood, the Lord Despenser, or Chancellor of the Exchequer. 'The Hell-Fire Club' had included such famous names as the Earl of Sandwich and Sir John Wilkes, the Secretary of the Navy. It even had been visited by Benjamin Franklin, himself no mean scholar of magic.

Ward's circle, or as I suspected his 'coven', met at Cliveden on the Astors' Thameside estate, and the accompanying scandal of the bizarre sex orgies that took place there, under Ward's aegis, but presumably unknown to the Astors, brought down John Profumo, who was then the Secretary of Defence. This unfortunate man later spent many years in the East End of London, working for the under-privileged in soup kitchens, presumably to 'Expiate his Sin', as some media sources nauseatingly implied. What a dreadfully old-fashioned way of looking at that unfortunate man's alleged sexual indiscretions. Incidentally, his unselfish dedication to social work, in the East End, eventually earned him a well-deserved knighthood, under a subsequent Labour government.

But the facts are plain. John Profumo, because he was a Cabinet Minister in Macmillan's government, had been destroyed politically, and the Conservative government had been brought down, in the sixties, in much the same way that years later, in the seventies, the political and private reputations of Jeremy Thorpe, the one-time Liberal leader, also were massacred by the media.

Allowing for some minor differences, it is evident that John Profumo, Stephen Ward, and Jeremy Thorpe were all victims of savage psychic attacks, as well as public ones.

The well-manipulated Profumo scandal, allegedly involving him with Christine Keeler, who coincidentally was alleged to have shared her affections with a Captain Ivanov of the Russian KGB, was fully and sanctimoniously reported, with great relish, by the media and especially by the newly liberated BBC.

With accomplished skill, political commentators dissected and destroyed John Profumo's professional career for ever, and this certainly helped to bring down the Conservative government at the next election.

It was a triumph of vicious propaganda that never, for one moment, questioned the validity of the circumstances leading up to the unfortunate Minister's alleged involvement with Christine Keeler. It also never questioned why the KGB had allowed one of their operatives to sleep with a British 'call-girl' (as she was described) who could, presumably, also have been employed by MI6 in order to discredit, or even blackmail, a KGB agent.

Although the Russians supposedly disciplined Captain Ivanov, and shipped him back home, it is obvious that his actions actually must have had the full approval of the KGB. Otherwise, he would have been severely punished, if not executed, for having been involved in such decadent bourgeois practices.

In fact, during Lord Denning's subsequent summing-up of the evidence, relating to the Profumo case, which had been brought before him as a member of the Royal Commission set up for this purpose, this level-headed and impartial judge described certain photographic evidence, as nearly as I can remember his words: 'In all my years in the judiciary, I have never seen more disgusting and degrading evidence, and therefore, in the public interest, I strongly recommend that it should be destroyed;' or words to that effect.

Apparently, much of this evidence was pornographic, the extraordinary photographs having been taken in near-darkness, using *infra-red film*, a fact presumably unknown to the participants in these alleged sex orgies.

These bizarre proceedings took place at the large country cottage, at Cliveden, leased by Stephen Ward, who had become the key figure in the scandal.

At this time, 1963, infra-red techniques were rarely used privately, indicating that the pictures, seemingly, were taken for purposes of blackmail, most probably by the KGB.

But despite Lord Denning's recommendations, this photographic evidence was not destroyed. I have been told that it eventually found its way into the Cabinet files of the Labour Party. If that is true, it would be interesting to know who countermanded the Chief Justice's official recommendations.

In another more recent example of political psychic attack, in this case against the ex-leader of the Liberal Party, Jeremy Thorpe, the media first helped him to gain a powerful public following through his many sympathetic appearances on television and radio, and then a few years later gleefully assisted in his political destruction.

It all started during the run-up to the election of Harold Wilson's second term of office in power.

Thorpe had been elected the leader of the Liberal Party and the media appeared to set out to prove that here was a political giant in the making.

During his election campaign Thorpe never seemed to be off the small screen, which did everything in its power to show him off to his best advantage.

He came across to the viewers as witty and charming, with a razor-sharp mind and such acute political awareness, that it was almost as if he knew the content of the questions, which were being put to him by various television commentators. It certainly looked as though Jeremy Thorpe could not put a foot wrong, and soon he was riding the crest of a political wave.

The only other politician to shine during that campaign was Harold Wilson, who already was a very polished television performer, showing no sign of the unease and insecurity which he exhibited on television in later years.

Edward Heath could not measure up to either of these two outstanding television personalities, as they

181

appeared to be in the skilled hands of their presenters on the media.

By the time the election was covered by an excited staff on BBC television, the result was hardly in doubt. Although Harold Wilson and the Labour government scraped home with a small majority, Jeremy Thorpe's Liberal Party polled an astonishing *six million votes*, more than half the total votes for either of the other two parties.

The remarkable thing about the result, was that the Liberal Party only consisted of *thirteen* members of Parliament, whereas Labour and Tories numbered over six hundred MPs between them, yet these two other parties each had only polled about twice the number of Liberal votes.

It was, virtually, a triumph for Thorpe and the Liberals.

It was also a frightening demonstration of the power of the medium of television.

The only time I have ever witnessed anything like it was in the United States, years later, when I saw Ronald Reagan wipe Jimmy Carter off the screens, in that historic television debate which was seen by an estimated American audience of over a hundred million people.

This latter result had little to do with Reagan's political expertise, but a great deal to do with his performing talent and his undoubted ability as a communicator. He also had been briefed, brilliantly.

It was a remarkable performance by any standard, but at the time it made me feel uneasy, because it certainly helped to put Ronald Reagan into the White House. It was virtually election by television!

Understandably in Jeremy Thorpe's case he had been overwhelmed by the unbelievably successful outcome of the election. It was a very human reaction. Personable, witty and charming, the Liberal leader shone forth in all his glory.

However, this had not sat too well with the other political parties, because so close was the small majority of the Labour Party in that election that it could only gain

182

a working majority *if* the Liberals threw their weight of thirteen votes behind whatever motion the Labour government wished to push through.

Suddenly, Jeremy Thorpe found himself in a position of considerable power. Both sides were eager to woo him for his favour.

I believe that had he been more malleable in responding to Harold Wilson's persuasive overtures, when the crunch finally came for him and the Liberal leader found himself in dire trouble, through his alleged personal indiscretions, left-wing sympathizers in the media might have been willing to help him.

This left-wing influence in the BBC, at that time, had become much increased because the younger members of the media, whom Carleton Greene had pressed to the front of television reporting and light entertainment satire, were mainly left-wing socialists. In fact, it seemed that Greene had deliberately chosen these specially selected young 'Turks', fresh from the major universities, and especially from Oxford and Cambridge, to carry out his plans for the BBC.

This domination of the News and Current Affairs Department of the Corporation, by graduates from the two leading British universities, was not a new thing. For years the BBC, then mainly radio, had been known as the 'Oxbridge Mafia', even before Carleton Greene took over, but in those days these graduates were Liberals rather than left-wing radicals.

Certainly, the Director General's young team of satirists, in the new radical image of BBC's light entertainment, was now dominated by gifted amateur comedians, most of them being drawn from the Cambridge Footlights and the Oxford University Dramatic Society (The OUDS), or culled from the fringes of the Edinburgh Festival. None of them, to my knowledge, was ever right-wing in their political views.

This was the situation in the media, as far as the BBC was concerned, when Jeremy Thorpe was rocketed to power, but Carleton Greene had left the Corporation by the time the Liberal leader found himself suddenly faced with political and personal disaster.

In Thorpe's case this was due to a nationwide scandal, alleging his involvement with homosexual acts, which led to a man threatening to publicize their alleged relation-ship. Further allegations stated that the Liberal leader had agreed to a colleague arranging a bizarre attempt to silence this man in the course of which his dog had been shot and killed.

The whole extraordinary story read like the script of the most fanciful television soap opera!

Abruptly the media, which had played such an important part in Jeremy Thorpe's rise to power, now turned on him and viciously tore his personal and public reputations to shreds, without showing any mercy.

It was one of the most unpleasant episodes I have ever witnessed on television, radio, and in most of the British Press, and for me it was a further demonstration of one meaning of the words: 'Psychic Attack'. For here was a direct attack on the mind, or, if you prefer it, the soul of Jeremy Thorpe.

The whole campaign of attack could indeed be described as 'soul-destroying', and the treatment of the Jeremy Thorpe affair by the media, like the earlier Profumo case, was a sickening display of self-righteous hypocrisy.

In Harold Wilson's perceptive words: 'A week is a long time in politics.'

Like many others, I was sickened by such cavalier treatment of a former public figure.

So far, I have been discussing the validity of psy-chological warfare, or, as it is now known, psychological operations, and in this realm of such attacks on the mind, there are two main areas of expertise.

The first is in the political arena and the second is purely commercial, though one can argue that the two are so inextricably mixed as to be facets of the same thing. However, for our purposes, these two major forms of psychic attack can be regarded as separate entities.

Let us now examine the commercial application of psychological operations.

During the past forty years, I have fronted a number of top-level commercial conferences, ranging from pharmaceutical companies, engaged in the production of cough-medicines, to computer manufacturers, frozen-food processors, industrial groups, investment houses, and plastics firms. I have helped to launch new tooth-pastes, Nylon panty-hose, and just about every other facet of commercial enterprise, as well.

At these functions, I have always asked to sit-in at the preliminary briefings, to get the feel of the product or enterprise and in every case I have listened to someone, usually the sales manager, or marketing expert, giving a pep-talk on the psychological aspect of the sales campaign.

I have also heard professional psychologists, at certain conferences, speak about these matters. In other words, I have seen the launching of many subtle, and not so subtle, psychic attacks on the minds of the public.

Even the way that these conferences are set up is in keeping with the principles of 'mind-conditioning', for the whole thrust of these conferences is invariably calculated to generate confidence and enthusiasm among the delegates, especially the sales staff.

Usually, I am brought in to give the whole proceedings a flavour of humour and, normally, I am instructed to perform my services as Master of Ceremonies, Court Jester, or even as a valid Presenter, but in a lighter vein, to take the heaviness out of the cake.

During my years of being involved in this sort of commercial enterprise, I have discovered a fascinating truth.

Only when the conference is presented with an audio-visual emphasis, especially by the use of television recordings specifically made for the occasion, does the full impact of the proceedings sink deeply into the unconscious mind of the delegates.

In other words, the whole set-up of each conference, in which I have played a tactical part, has been designed as an all-out, psychological attack on the minds of the delegates, with the public as the end target.

I must digress here and explain why I believe that television, as a medium of manipulation, is so effective.

In 1944, when I was instructing a group of airmen from the American 8th Air Force, I was told to get across to these young members of Aircrew the importance of *instant* aircraft recognition. This vital need was occasioned by the shooting-down, in disastrous numbers, of the escorting Allied fighter-planes, during the mass American daylight air-raids on Europe.

Understandably, in the excitement and terror of the frequent air battles, when hundreds of German fighters attacked the huge formations of Flying Fortresses and Liberators (B17s and B24s), the many air-gunners aboard each aircraft only had a few seconds to determine whether the fighter approaching them was friend or foe.

In the mêlée of air-fighting, the gunners played safe and fired at everything that did not, like their own aircraft, have four engines. The results became a major problem, when too many Allied fighters were shot down by the planes they were escorting.

Among others, I was pulled out of my regular job, which at that time was briefing operational aircrew for attacks against Europe, to try to remedy this chaotic state of affairs.

The instrument I used, to teach aircraft recognition, was an ingenious adaptation of an ordinary Epidiascope. It projected large pictures of three-way views of different Allied fighters, with the modification of an adjustable camera-shutter, which projected the image for varying time-exposures, ranging from a minute to a five-hundredth of a second.

It was very difficult to hold the aircrews' attention and, in spite of my turning these sessions into a betting competition for beer-money, which the young Americans enjoyed, their concentration was inclined to wander.

The results were abysmal! Until one morning, when a fault developed in the machine and a flickering effect from a loose connection became apparent.

It was as though a miracle had occurred! Abruptly, the results rose, from a dismal 10 per cent to nearly 100 per cent correct identification, even when I closed the timing device of the shutter on the Epidiascope, so that the images only appeared for a mere fraction of second.

It was, of course, the *flickering effect* that was causing a focus of attention on the images and routeing them straight through to the unconscious minds of the watching airmen. It seemed as though they were being hypnotized by the flickering light, which is a classic technique used in hypnotherapy.

My flight-sergeant was all for correcting the fault, but, fortunately, I told him we had not got time to do so. It was only afterwards that I realized what had happened.

Suddenly, I remembered my childhood, when I had so enjoyed the great comedians of the silent movies. I realized that I could recall each visual gag, in every silent comedy film I had ever seen.

I also remembered the nickname we had given to those early films. We had called them: the 'Flicks', because of the flickering effect of the projectors.

Using a stop-watch, I tried to work out the timing of this flickering effect of the faulty connection in the Epidiascope. As near as I could figure it, the cyclic rate varied between sixteen and eighteen flickers a second, the same speed as that of the early movie-projectors.

I was so impressed that I mentioned the incident to my superiors, but they ignored it.

However, the results spoke for themselves. By sheer accident, I had found a solution to the problem of almost instantaneous aircraft recognition. At least, the

American air-gunners, whom I trained by this method, would make far less mistakes in their air-to-air combat.

Incidentally, when the addition of sound altered the speed of movie projection, to a rate of approximately twenty-five frames a second, the same flickering effect was present, but it was less obvious and, therefore, easier to watch.

Nevertheless it had the same effect on cinema goers, implanting the screen images so firmly in their unconscious minds that international movie stars became famous, almost overnight.

Today, the television images are scanned at the rate of 24.9 frames a second, and the results are obvious to anyone who watches the small screen.

The psychological effect is so powerful that, over the past forty years, a huge, world-wide industry has sprung up, involving the expenditure of billions, in hard currencies, for advertising, propaganda, sport and entertainment.

To paraphrase Karl Marx, once more: 'Television is the Opiate of the Masses.'

We next come to the part of this chapter which you may find the hardest to accept.

Can there be a psychic attack, without all the machinery of the Press and the complex instrumentation of the rest of the media?

From my own experiences and those of others, I would say: 'Yes! I am sure this type of mental attack against the individual can be made!'

For instance we all know, or have read about mental cruelty having been the reason for many divorces. This is only one example of another sort of psychic attack, in which a persistently negative attitude, on the part of one marriage partner, can cause great suffering to the other party involved.

In her book, delightfully entitled *Psychic Self-Defence*, Dion Fortune (the pen-name of a clever and honest researcher into the paranormal) tells of her early experience of an actual psychic attack, which left her with a nervous breakdown, and put her under psychiatric care, for over two years.

I strongly recommend that you read this fascinating book, but I will paraphrase this example from her work.

Dion Fortune started her professional life as a young teacher in a training establishment for women, and soon found herself involved with an unpleasant situation, when one of the other young teachers fell foul of their employer, an exceptionally strong-willed woman, whom they nicknamed, the 'warden'.

Miss Fortune befriended the unhappy girl, who was terrified, and was warned by her to leave the school as soon as she could, because their employer was evil!

Having seen a few instances of this formidable woman, wielding her undoubted power, without consideration for those whom she was manipulating, Dion Fortune decided to hand in her notice.

Unwisely, as she admits in her book, while waiting for her taxi to arrive, she decided to go into the 'warden's' office and tell her a few home truths.

It was a terrible mistake, and though she only retained the haziest memory of what happened in that room, two hours later she was in a state of complete mental collapse.

This wasn't just a case of a nervous youngster being pitted against an experienced professional teacher, for Miss Fortune was a strong-willed and highly intelligent woman, even at that age. Furthermore, she was certain that she had right on her side, and she was not lacking in any way in self-confidence.

Yet, within a couple of hours, which for the rest of her life remained a near blank, her employer, who was obviously an accomplished hypnotist and an unscrupulous mind-manipulator, virtually destroyed all her junior teacher's confidence. In that short time she reduced her from being a healthy young woman, to a case for a convalescent home, where she eventually had to be sent, suffering from a complete nervous collapse.

That is an extraordinary, but by no means rare case of psychic attack, without the use of any power except that of the human mind.

The more you think about it, the more frightening it becomes.

Because of her dreadful experience, Miss Fortune pursued a long course of study of the paranormal, or, as it was called in those days: the occult. A fine, natural scholar, this clever woman was ideally equipped, physically and mentally, once she had recovered from that terrible experience, to tackle the long hard study and stern self-discipline required to qualify as a ritual magician, which, as well as emerging as a successful authoress, she eventually became.

During her adventurous lifetime, Dion Fortune was also a prominent member of the 'Golden Dawn', that extraordinary group of ritual magicians, drawn from various walks of life. These were mainly men, like Doctor Westcott, a London coroner; Doctor Woodard, another physician; Lidell Mathers, a fine linguist, with a deep knowledge of dead languages; his rival, Aleister Crowley, the adroit poet, scholar and mountaineer; William Butler Yeats, the famous poet; Sir Gerald Kelly, the Royal Academician and portraitist; and a number of other eminent seekers after the Gnosis, including the authors, Arthur Machen and Algernon Blackwood.

This intelligent woman's knowledge of the workings of the mind, and its application to scholarship and research, especially when undertaking mental journeys into the realms of the imagination and the depths of the unconscious mind, has given us some fascinating books, including one on the Cabala which is both understandable and informative.

Though I would never recommend anyone to pursue the path of the ritual-magician, because it is intended only for those with an exceptionally strong will, and a rock-hard steadiness of purpose and mental equilibrium, I would encourage any seeker after knowledge to read Dion Fortune's books and also those of W. E. Butler, a knowledgeable scholar and a well-balanced commentator on these strange pathways of the mind.

Aleister Crowley's books I find to be too radical, though they are extremely well researched and academic to a degree, but, for me, they indicate much too perilous a path for ordinary mortals like myself to follow.

Crowley's own chaotic, drug-addicted lifestyle ended tragically in elderly obscurity, in Hastings. But not for long, because at his funeral, in Hove, there was a public row over the pagan rites performed by his friends, when his erotic 'Hymn to Pan' was chanted. Crowley's lifestyle should serve as a horrific warning to anyone who tries to follow his peculiarly individual path towards the abyss of insanity.

If anyone signed the Faustian Pact with his own conscience it was Aleister Crowley, who actively revelled in evil, thinking of himself as: 'The Great Beast' and who often signed his work with the numbers: 666. Crowley believed implicitly in the efficacy of psychic attack, and frequently employed magical rituals of the most destructive kind against his enemies, in the same way that he believed they were using similar black-magical methods to attack him.

In the course of one of these 'psychic battles', which took place before the First World War, between Aleister Crowley and his rival Lidell Mathers, both their residences, Crowley's in Scotland and Mathers' in Paris, became virtually uninhabitable. This evidently was due to the continual 'poltergeist' type of terrifying physical manifestations which filled the two houses with loudly banging doors, dreadful smells, terrifying apparitions and intense feelings of hostility and acute depression, which inside Crowley's house, Boleskine Manor, on the shores of Loch Ness, allegedly still lingers on.

Dion Fortune's fascinating book, *Psychic Self-Defence*, has much interesting information about different types of psychic attack and bears re-reading many times. It is most revealing and has run into many editions!

As for my own experiences of psychic attack, I have had enough bad times to convince me that these invisible and intangible assaults can and do exist. It even has been suggested, by reasonable and intelligent friends, that the loss of three of my adult children could have been as a direct result of concentrated ill-wishing. However, I do not agree.

Nevertheless, during my lifetime, I have come up against a number of patent manifestations of evil and, in overcoming them or by helping to upset their plans, my family and I may have become targets for such psychological assaults.

Certainly, Carleton Greene did much to hinder and hurt my career while I was at the BBC. However, that was in the terms of psychological operations, in which Sir Hugh was an expert.

I even found myself tagged by him and his associates with the name 'Fascist', which hardly applies, after all the years I have spent fighting that obscenity, not the least during the Second World War.

There is a cynical saying: 'Just because you are paranoid, doesn't mean they are not after you.'

When I told a few friends of my concern that harm was being done to my professional reputation, I sometimes got a sideways look and the hint that I might be suffering from paranoia.

I am too much of a realist, in the tough, practical world of show-business to have time for that phobia, but, as far as some of my 'friends' were concerned, it was a neat way of avoiding the unpleasantness of the issue, and, at the same time, an excuse for not helping me to do something about it.

As I have pointed out, these psychological attacks are very difficult to prove. Anyway, all that aggravation is in the past. I have only mentioned it in the book to show, from bitter experience, how effective I have found such psychological attacks can prove to be.

Which brings me to the type of psychic attack that is the hardest of all to accept, especially by those whose minds are firmly closed.

This type of spiritual assault is usually described under the blanket terms of 'Black Magic', Voodoo, Ju-Ju, Obeah, Magumba, 'Pointing the Bone', and other names and terms, used in destructive witchcraft.

The methods used by witchdoctors and Shamans have been well publicized by the sensational press and documented by writers of horror stories, but their actual effect is not acceptable to, nor believed in, by the Western mind.

But those who have lived in Africa, Australia, South America, the West and East Indies, the Orient, and other remote parts of the world, know that these destructive 'astral' attacks do exist and are much feared.

My late father-in-law, a wise and logically-minded Scot, a scientist, veterinarian and doctor, with an excellent academic background and nerves of steel, who had lived for over sixty years in Central and East Africa, told me that he would never allow his hair-cuttings, nail-clippings, or soiled underwear to fall into the hands of a witchdoctor, in case of such an attack being launched against him.

Whether uninformed Western minds scoff at it or not, such attacks using methods like 'Pointing the Bone' are fully authenticated and well documented among those who work with the Aborigines, in Australia.

Furthermore, the effectiveness of Voodoo dolls in the hands of adept West Indian Houngans also has been well researched and found to be frighteningly valid. Even if all these cases could be explained away by the principles of modern psychiatry, the results are still frightening.

These occurrences are by no means rare. In fact, there is too much valid material, provided by able and qualified observers who have lived for long periods of time in those parts of the world where these paranormal activities manifest, to ignore all the evidence.

Nevertheless, those who have not travelled extensively except on package holidays, prefer to dismiss the existence of such things and try to explain them away as paranoia!

It shows how much things have changed that, as I mentioned, with the loss of my three much-loved children, a rather different attitude to my own family's tragic misfortunes has emerged among some of our friends.

To satisfy the most pressing of these my wife and I had ourselves blessed by our good friend, the late Dom Robert Petitpierre, the long-time exorcist of the Church of England, who had no doubt whatsoever that I was suffering from such an attack.

He explained to me that it probably was connected with the extraordinary efforts I had been forced to make during my long investigation, with the help of Special Branch, into my son Gus's death in an air crash.

For the present, let it suffice that because of personal experiences I believe in the effectiveness of these attacks on the mind, or soul, and that there are ways to avoid, ameliorate, or even to abort them.

All these defensive measures require an open mind which can think powerful *positive* thoughts and, thereby, defend the person under psychic/psychological attack against the current of evil, i.e. the electro-chemically induced transmission of *negative* energy caused by ill-wishing which deliberately is being projected against them by another hostile mind.

In such cases the negative (evil) force sent against you, invariably, seems to return to the originator of psychic attack. I am convinced that this is the true meaning of the phrase: '*Honi soit qui mal y pense!*' 'Evil be to him (or her), who Evil thinks!'.

Whatever the case may be, I can only recommend that once a person has good reason to believe that a psychic assault, in any form, is being or has been made against him, or her, the first thing to do is to pinpoint the source of the negative force, and the method being used, be it in the form of a libellous or slanderous rumour being spread by someone, or whether it is an actual campaign being waged against you by an individual, a group, or by some powerful person in business, politics, or within the media.

Bearing in mind the ever-present danger that it is easy to become paranoic about such things, a trustworthy and open-minded friend should be informed of your suspicions, as soon as possible, with the object of checking up to see if your fears are valid, or are just the products of an unreasoning anxiety.

If the results of that impartial investigation indicate that there is indeed a source of such malevolence being directed against you, in any of the ways that I have described in this chapter, the sooner you confront the issue head-on the better. When left alone, in the hope that this sort of evil will go away, things will only get worse.

The residue of the sort of psychological attack, that I suffered from during the Carleton Greene regime, stayed with me for a long time and echoes of it even now still exist.

Several acquaintances, who were directly influenced against me from this source, have since apologized to me for harbouring such thoughts. Which only goes to show that the sooner you become aware of such an attack the better.

A positive attitude, together with a firm refusal to be overcome by fear or panic, is still your best protection, and I certainly do not discount prayer as one of your strongest defences, and by all means consult a priest, rabbi, clergyman, or an open-minded psychiatrist, if you feel you cannot cope with the problem alone.

Today, more than ever before, it is imperative that those with open minds should maintain constant vigilance against this sort of mental assault and other negative forms of psychic/psychological operations.

It is as much a part of survival as any other kind of awareness, by which, so far, we have maintained our position as the dominant species on our planet.

CHAPTER NINE

Places of the heart

There is a well-worn cliché: 'Home is where the heart is'.

This maxim is dismissed too often, and too lightly, for the words contain a remarkable truth.

Undoubtedly, there are places where a sensitive individual feels at home. In such locations, the open-minded person senses tranquillity, and a feeling of belonging and well-being. Certain sites can arouse emotional excitement, which often accompanies a creative endeavour, such as original writing, expressionist sculpture, imaginative thinking, musical composition, and just about every other branch of the arts.

I call these sites: places of the heart.

In 1976, I entered the fascinating world of the dowsers, through my friendship with Colin and David Bloy and their open-minded colleagues. They, painstakingly, taught me the rudiments of the use of the forked twig, the angle-rods, the pendulum and the rest of the simple instrumentation of the art of the dowser/diviner, and opened my mind to more new horizons of thought.

It was an exciting time!

This was because this group of intelligent dowsers, most of whom were qualified practitioners in many branches of the professions, such as surveying and architecture, engineering, medicine, and physics, were engaged, individually and collectively, in trying to pin down the validity, or otherwise, of the existence of fields and lines of force, which appeared to be part of an invisible and intangible grid, criss-crossing Britain.

They told me they believed that a similar type of energy-grid existed, possibly, over the whole of the earth, in the form of a recognizable pattern, detectable by dowsing.

Sounds crazy, doesn't it?

Not if you remember that lines of geo-magnetic force which are also intangible and invisible, but which, nevertheless, exist and can be measured, cover our planet in a recognizable pattern, which is in the process of being charted by professional geo-physicists working for oil companies and universities.

The emergent study of geo-magnetism and the existence of gravito-magnetic fields and lines of force and their effect on all life on our planet, has lately been given credence, although research into their properties has only been undertaken by the Establishment within the last twenty years.

One must also remember that the scientific Establishment already accepts, as a convention, that the earth is covered by an invisible, intangible, network of lines, by which we navigate our way, by land, sea, and air.

We call these lines the parallels of longitude and latitude.

Yet, this archetypal grid, which occupies an exact, measurable, location on the surface of the earth, and its oceans, actually *does not exist*, but it is of immense importance to us and to the safety of any lengthy journey that we undertake.

Moreover, we have, for centuries, built many extensive systems and grids across various sections of our planet. These networks, range from underground irrigation-channels, like those of the ancient Persian system of wells and connecting subterranean canals, called the 'Fahjan', through the Roman Empire's vast system of aqueducts and overland irrigation-ditches, to the modern, above- and below-ground, oil and gas pipelines, and electricity cable systems.

We also endure the presence of those ubiquitous, ugly

metal pylons, that carry the power of alternating-current over a large part of the civilized world.

The object of this particular team of dowsers, of which the Bloy brothers were prominent members, was to chart the existence of what have become known as 'ley-lines'.

Put simply, some dowsers believe that these invisible lines of force are generated, originally, by crystalline mineral masses, contained in rock formations, and are then channelled along the tracks of the maze of underground water-courses, which criss-cross our planet.

A very extensive system of these water channels, both *above* and *below* ground, cover the British Isles, acting as a natural drainage system for the enormous quantity of rainwater that constantly falls on these islands.

The dowsers, who are engaged in this search to chart the subterranean water courses, believe that powerful lines of detectable, but invisible, *above-ground* force, are often reflections of these subterranean pipelines.

Moreover, they believe that these overland lines of force, the so-called 'ley-lines', can be manipulated, much in the same way that conventional electrical current is controlled by huge transformers and massive switching gear.

They also believe that this knowledge was arcane, that our ancestors were well aware of its potential, and that Stone Age priests and wise-men did, in fact, use the 'ley system' for their own purposes, even though they probably did not understand how the system worked!

That also sounds crazy, until you recall that, even in our present state-of-art of technology, we do *not* yet possess anywhere near full knowledge of the power that we have named: electricity, from the ancient Greek word: electron.

Most of my adult life, I have used grids of different sorts to help me find my way around the world, as a keen amateur sailor, a flier, and as a seeker after knowledge. These grids, on charts and maps, have ranged from conventional latitude and longitude, based on Mercator's projection, to air-charts, for flight-navigation, showing the convention of invisible air corridors for safe air traffic regulation.

I also have used radio-navigation charts, showing the position of other *invisible* lines of force, which can be picked up by a suitable instrument and then 'strobed', i.e. turned into a static picture on a cathode-ray tube display, or, alternatively, shown as a digital LED read-out.

With modern systems of accurate air and surface navigation, based on inertial-guidance systems and other sophisticated techniques, for finding the traveller's exact position, I have come to accept the existence of all these *invisible and intangible lines, even when they only exist as a convention in the mind*.

In other words, these lines only exist in our imagination, and are, therefore, archetypal images of the human collective unconscious, or as I see them, images of the universal overmind.

Yet, they are absolutely real and valid in every way, and we trust millions of lives every day to our airways' navigational systems. These are based on the existence of various *imaginary grids*, even though they do not actually exist, other than as a pictorial representation of *invisible, but detectable, radio transmissions*!

How crazy can the Establishment get, according to its *own* standards of disbelief? Having said that, let me explain, how I came to accept the valid existence of these so-called 'ley-lines'.

Put at its simplest, I dowsed them, detecting the course of their progress, both above and below ground, until I was assured of the validity of their presence, and later I saw other dowsers, who were not aware of the results of my own dowsing, proceed to follow *exactly* the same course that I had previously and unknown to them, marked out for myself.

Frankly, it shook me rigid!

At this point, let me set the record straight about the difference between the terminology of 'ley-lines' and 'leys'.

'Leys' are the names given to observed lines-of-sight, apparently denoting the presence of ancient trackways, observed between objects, such as large marker-stones, specially sited dew-ponds, church spires, and deliberate modifications to prominent points on the skyline. All of which once was used to indicate the line of a straight track or 'ley', as they were named by Arthur Watkins, a twentieth-century businessman and amateur scholar, widely experienced in the geography and topography of his native county, Herefordshire.

One day, before the First World War, Watkins was riding along a hill crest, overlooking the Bredwardine valley, one of the most picturesque vales in Britain, when, in a sudden flash of intuition, he seemed to see, subjectively, a grid made up of lines of light, supposedly much like our present-day laser beams, laid out on the valley floor below him.

These lines seemed to him to connect prominent landmarks, such as I have described above, apparently indicating the presence of straight trackways, like the ancient Roman roads, but of a *far older* origin.

Watkins was so impressed by his subjective experience, that, with his methodical mind and original thinking, for he had already invented the light-meter used in photography, he proceeded to develop his theory by walking along these indicated tracks.

Many of these he had to uncover in part, for they had been hidden for centuries, beneath grass and undergrowth. Nevertheless, he was able to prove that they had existed.

Moreover, by using large-scale maps and a ruler and compass Arthur Watkins was able to detect the presence of a whole system of these ancient trackways.

He did this by connecting prominent landmarks on National Survey charts, and projecting the resultant straight line for some considerable mileage, passing through other large objects such as a barrow, a tumulus, or a stone dolmen. These leys could then be verified by walking the length of them in physical confirmation of their existence.

Watkins only accepted the possibility of the existence of a 'ley' when he could ascertain, on survey charts of the largest possible scale, that more than ten prominent objects, such as church spires, tumuli, barrows and other ancient earth mounds, dolmens, dew-ponds, etc., were in alignment, over a distance of some miles.

Only then would he consider walking the 'ley', thereby confirming, or negating, his findings. In fact, he became so adept at detecting these ancient trackways, that his proportion of hits far exceeded his few misses.

Convinced that he had stumbled across an ancient truth, Watkins published a book on his discoveries, in 1922, and called it: *Early British Trackways.* He followed this work with another, published in 1925, called *The Old Straight Track.*

They are both modest and sensible works, obviously the product of a clear-thinking mind, and illustrated by Watkins' own excellent photographs. These clearly show what his thesis is about. The books are well worth reading and contain some fascinating ideas. They are evidently the work of painstaking research, by an honest and open-minded man.

When they were published, they caused quite a stir. They were, predictably, condemned as rubbish by the archaeological Establishment, who were furious that an *amateur* should dare to put forward a theory, that they had not conceived.

This controversy and the popularity of his second book among imaginative readers brought about the formation of the Old Straight Track Society. This lasted up to the start of the Second World War, and was revived, post-war, in its present, unofficial, existence, by enthusiastic groups of 'ley-hunters' who have developed Watkins' original thesis into a far more complex practice, or, if you prefer it, art.

This is where the confusion comes in, namely in the

difference between Watkins' definition of 'leys', and the modern hunt for 'ley-lines'.

To recap; the definition of 'leys', refers to physically confirmable ancient trackways, which usually are first plotted on large-scale survey maps, and then walked along their length to ascertain their validity, or otherwise.

'Ley-lines' on the other hand are similar in their concept to 'Dragon-lines,' which prominently feature in the ancient Chinese art of Feng-Shui (pronounced Fung-Shway), meaning 'wind and water', the two great forces that form the landscape. Feng-Shui is also the name given to the ancient art of Chinese landscaping, and landscape painting.

This Oriental definition refers to invisible lines of force, beneficial or otherwise, positive or negative, which Chinese diviners, along with many hundreds of millions of Chinese people, believe exist in the form of lines of 'Dragon force', which they call: Lung-Mei (pronounced Lung May).

These Dragon-lines, *supposedly*, carry the subtle energies of Yin and Yang, the archetypal forces that are symbolized in this figure:

It is of interest to note, that the areas of black and white, representing light and darkness, in this circular symbol, are *exactly* equal in size. This is because the Chinese concept of the existence of Yin and Yang is similar to that of the Manichaean Heresy, with its belief that Good and Evil are equally interdependent, so that each of these forces can only be expressed in terms of the other.

Recently, Bob Cowley, another good friend and a valid researcher into Arthur Watkins' theories, came up with the interesting information that Watkins was a sensitive, and had seen, *clairvoyantly*, the original lines of light, which he wisely described as a product of his imagination. Which of course, in essence, is what it was.

I have had similar experiences, when I have been dowsing for these lines of force, some of which must have been generated in the universal overmind, by the very fact of their existence in the minds of the hundreds of thousands of travellers in the distant past, who once walked or rode along these ancient trackways.

I already have related how, as a boy, I used to sit beside the old Ham Street Roman Road, high above the Romney Marsh, and watch in my imagination the long flow of history that so richly mantles this lovely part of Kent.

The Chinese, who paralleled Ancient Egypt with their own complex civilization of sophistication and knowledge for almost three millennia, believed that the shape and form of the skyline and the layout of the environment determined the fate of the people, who lived in its ambience.

Just as the Egyptians, the Assyrians, the Persians, and, later, the Greeks, Romans and Arabian civilizations carefully planned and laid out their cities, designing their homes to a specific 'Canon of Proportion', so the Chinese, from circa 1300 BC, have been engaged in the detailed planning of their environment.

This reached its peak at the end of the Ching Dynasty, when the Great Chinese Revolution, of 1912, took place and the reign of the monarchic dynasties ended.

The ancient art of 'town and country planning' which after the fall of the Roman empire was lost to Britain for centuries, has always been a dominant factor in Chinese life. Moreover, the criteria for the detailed rules governing the conservation of the ecology and ethology of China have been encapsulated, for well over two thousand years, in the art of China's Feng-Shui diviners.

These wise surveyor/magicians, working with their Feng-Shui compasses and dowsing instruments, were virtually a combination of landscape-gardeners, engineers, architects, and even interior decorators.

Their job was to determine the exact layout of the environment, so that all the different factors, within its parameters, should not interfere with the free flow of the subtle forces, which they believed were being generated by the environment.

That may seem to be impractical Oriental mumbo-jumbo, to those who know nothing of the Chinese mentality, but even my amateur acquaintance with Chinese arts and crafts, and my two visits to Hong Kong, have opened my eyes to the extraordinary sophistication and extreme practicality of these very remarkable people.

Recently, Japan has been the recipient of great admiration and the respect of the Western world, for its dramatic resurgence into a powerful economic and technological power in the world, following total defeat by the Western Alliance.

Yet, the history of this ingenious nation is only a pale reflection of that of the great dynasties of China, who had reached a pinnacle of civilization when the Japanese were still in a state of semi-barbarism.

For me, Japan has represented the Spartan civilization of Ancient Greece, with its emphasis on war and the martial arts, whereas China seems more like Athens with all the Athenian love of the arts, crafts and sciences.

Japan, with its code of the Samurai, has a teutonic, militaristic background, which, latterly, drew it into the Axis alliance with Nazi Germany; a perfect example of 'like attracting like'.

China, on the other hand, throughout the long and bloody Sino-Japanese war of the twenties, thirties and forties, maintained its historical image and character, even though the dynasties had been supplanted by Sun

205

Yat-sen's great revolution in 1912, which turned China into a republic.

Both nations use much the same alphabet and characters, though the languages are different, and both peoples use Feng-Shui diviners, to help them lay out the landscape and even the interiors of their homes, in accordance with the ancient canon of proportion of this arcane art which the West has, contemptuously, labelled a 'pseudo-science'.

During the Chinese Communist revolution, this ancient art fell into disrepute, as it clashed with Marxist materialism and, at one time, Feng-Shui was forbidden, much in the same way that the Holy Bible is a restricted import into Soviet Russia, except as a personal item belonging to visitors, who must take it with them when they leave.

Nevertheless, in present-day China, as well as in Hong Kong, Singapore, and Taiwan, the art of divinatory Feng-Shui has regained much of its lost influence, and once again Chinese town and country planning and even the arrangement of the interiors of individual houses, is being laid out according to its ancient tenets.

How then does the Feng-Shui diviner practise his profession?

Basically the art itself is a mixture of intuition, tradition, astrology, a definitive canon of proportion, and commonsense.

It takes many years of apprenticeship and study, for the practitioner to learn all the complexities of Feng-Shui, which primarily are determined by the earth's relationship with the sun, moon and planets, its contemporary position in the zodiac, the shape and form of the local skyline, the natural topography of the surrounding landscape, and the addition of any man-made modifications, already imposed on the environment by previous inhabitants.

The ancient Chinese were also great astronomers, using their accurate observations of the heavens and local environmental conditions as the focus for their interpretation of each situation, much in the same way

206

that present-day meteorologists determine long-range weather-forecasting.

Therefore, the position of the planets and the stellar constellations, and the seasonal changes of climate and prevailing winds, etc., all played vital roles, according to the diviner, in the final determination of the correct placing, or modification, of each separate element, such as a house, a tomb, a pond, or stream, which was being built into the landscape.

Talking to Chinese scholars, who have made a deep study of Feng-Shui, leads me to believe in the efficacy of these methods, even in such overcrowded conditions as those of modern Hong Kong.

One factor that often struck me, as I walked along the streets of this exciting and teeming city, is that nobody seems to get in the way of anyone else, whereas, in contrast, a walk down Oxford Street in the centre of the West End of London, on a crowded shopping-day, is much more disturbing because of the jostling crowds constantly bumping into each other.

This factor is probably due to the Chinese love of Cosmos (Order), which is the result of millennia of their history. In fact, the history of China contains long periods of ordered life, interspersed with short periods of chaos, before a return to a new Cosmos takes place.

That is the natural progression of events, in any system or order of society that lasts for a significant length of time as a viable social entity.

This is self-evident in Chinese, Egyptian, Indian, South American, Persian, Greek, Roman and Spanish histories, where there were ordered civilizations, which endured by dynastic succession, sometimes for periods of hundreds of years, before decadence which is the natural process of entropic decay of any system, organic or inorganic, caused eventual chaos and the subsequent establishment of the new, conquering order.

It was the attempt, by Adolf Hitler and the Nazis, to introduce their Thousand Year Reich, without proper consideration of a correct and necessary methodology, other than by rapid military conquest, that led to the misery of the Second World War, and brought about the collapse and ruin of Germany.

Had the German National Socialist Workers' Party pursued their goal, in a more logical and democratic way, who knows what the end might have been? But with their crazy principles and perverted, hate-filled ideology that fuelled their chaotic crusade, the tragic conclusion was inevitable.

Only since post-war Western Germany has returned to a sane democratic system, has its amazing resurgence, economically, politically and morally, captured the grudging admiration of the rest of the world.

Modern Western Germany, which rose from the ruins of the collapse of the Third Reich, has been laid out in that cosmic sense of order, which is so dear to the Teutonic mind, with its love of: *Alles en Ordenung*.

In other words, the use of a form of Feng-Shui in the sense of town and country planning, and a careful reconsideration of the German ecology and its ethology, physically, spiritually and politically, has been employed in the rebuilding of the present-day democratic Federal Republic.

This is in contrast to the totalitarian East German Socialist Republic, which has precious little democracy in its present, political make-up, and itself is a satellite of Soviet Russia.

From such examples, we can see the importance of careful planning and consideration of *all* the environmental factors, in both ecological and ethological terms, which should go into the making of any social order.

Such were, and still are, the aims of the Chinese diviners.

The intricate techniques of this complex art allow for individual interpretation, by the practitioner of Feng-Shui, of all the observed factors in any landscaping or planning situation.

These are calculated and accurately orientated, by the use of compass and surveying-tube (an unsophisticated form of theodolite) and measured with silk cords, or bronze chains, for more exact results.

Pendulums are also used for dowsing the site, as well as for establishing the perpendicular, which probably is how the Ancient Egyptians used them. In addition, the aspect of the heavens, at the time of the survey, is accurately observed, just as it was in the past, by using a ritual jade disc (Pi) with a serrated edge to line up with certain key-configurations on the skyline. This was attached to a sighting tube (Tzung), made of bamboo, or laboriously drilled hard-stone, through which the stellar and planetary positions could be accurately observed, astronomically, and interpreted, astrologically.

At the same time, a careful survey of the whole district, using charts and dowsing, employing the forked twig and pendulum methods, established the position and flow, directionally, of all the complex system of subterranean water-channels in the area. Naturally this survey would also have involved the correct siting of any wells, which might be needed to ensure a supply of pure drinking water.

Basically, those were and still are, the actual techniques employed by the Feng-Shui diviners.

It is interesting that there were *no* female diviners employed in the past, and I understand that women still are not allowed to practise this art, even in modern China. I do not know why.

The diviners' art having evaluated all the physical and spiritual parameters i.e. social factors, within the local environment, the practitioner then must find the best compromise, commensurate with all the observations he has made of the whole situation. This of course means that he approaches the problem, *whollistically*.

Once again, apart from the employment of any para-normal factors involved in dowsing, and the practice of other divinatory elements in the survey, we can see a close parallel with all the logical elements used in present-day town and country planning.

I know a number of experienced surveyors and architects, involved in complex planning procedures, who use dowsing to help them evaluate their professional assessments of the results.

I assure you that the difference between Feng-Shui and modern social environmental planning is far less than one would imagine.

In the light of this surprising information, let us now consider how this applies to those individuals who wish to open their minds to the importance of the ecological and ethological factors governing the environment in which they live.

First, let us examine the case of those of us who live in the British Isles, though the same parameters seem to apply to anyone, living anywhere on the earth.

An assessment of our past history, especially that of the ancient civilizations of our early ancestors, will give us a clue to the importance of our own particular ecology and ethology. Along with a lot of other seekers after truth, I believe that we have to completely re-assess the primitive, 'unintelligent' image of what our early ancestors were like, and how they behaved.

We still do not know what specific purposes were served by the prehistoric construction of the six hundred, or so, stone circles and standing stones that dot our islands. But by the ingenious way in which they were erected, and because of the extraordinary accuracy of their siting and lay-out, according to Professor Alexander Thom, the distinguished Scottish scholar who has surveyed them, we must accept the fact that the builders of these extraordinary structures were far more intelligent than was previously supposed.

These weighty stone structures must have been erected for practical purposes considered to be worthwhile by their builders, in view of the enormous amount of effort and labour involved in their construction.

Our early ancestors were nothing if not practical, otherwise they would never have survived. Therefore, they must have had good reasons to spend *all* that time building these impressive megalithic monuments.

All of us, at some time in our lives, have felt the effect, pleasant and relaxing, or invigorating and stimulating, or, conversely, depressing and debilitating, of different places and sites, environments, landscapes, seascapes and, *especially*, skylines.

I am sure that many readers of this book will agree with me about the disturbing effect of much of the characterless, monotonous, post-war construction, of the high-rise apartments and office buildings, which often distort the skyline with their ill-considered ugliness. These have a deeply depressing effect on a large proportion of the people who have to live in their environment.

This is in contrast to the well-planned versions of some of the new towns, which have been built during the last few decades. But, sadly, the effect of the post-war Establishment attitude towards the over-riding importance of politically-motivated social architecture at any cost, in order to win mass votes, is all too apparent.

That is why I strongly oppose any overt, or covert, act by the Establishment, of *no matter what political persuasion*, to alter radically the environment, and *especially* the skyline, for their own purposes of personal profit, or for purely materialistic, or party-political motives.

Like many others, I am well aware of the traumatic effect that such radical modification of the landscape, environment and skyline can have upon my family, my friends and our posterity.

This is why, for me, 'Places of the Heart' are so important to identify, assess, and, if possible, enjoy, as a residence, temporary or otherwise.

Obviously, because of the tremendous effort and skilful hard work employed in the construction of our ancient stone circles, these places must also be considered to once have been, and in many cases still are 'Places of the Heart'.

As to why they were erected, my guess is that they were multi-purpose constructions, carefully sited for maximum significance and influence, for the benefit of *all* who were associated with them or living in their environment. They probably were also used as astronomical observatories, a theory supported by several eminent astronomers, like Professor Fred Hoyle, Doctor Hawkins, Doctor Krupp, and my friend, Doctor Patrick Moore.

The stone circles, which are very accurately laid-out, would probably have been employed in this role to determine the solstices and the equinoxes and to assess the correct times for planting, for the maximum yield of the crops.

The heavens provided the only clocks that our ancestors possessed, and their gnomons, or sun-clocks, using upright stones like obelisks to cast the solar shadow, plus carefully observed lunar and stellar positions, at their rise, zenith and fall below the skyline, were the surest methods our forefathers used for keeping an accurate track of time and the seasons.

Another possible use for these stone circles, horseshoe shapes, ellipses and equally carefully laid-out and constructed egg-shaped structures, was as a focus for all the different groups and tribes scattered about the area, within line-of-sight of them, thereby tending to give these diverse tribal elements a sense of belonging to a whole social entity, centred round the great stone structures.

It is also most likely that they were used as centres of worship, and in view of the habitual use of the stones by sick animals, which often lie beside the megaliths, where the grass seems to grow more lush, it is quite possible that the stones were used for healing purposes, as well.

Certainly, the megaliths seem to carry detectable charges of electricity, which can be verified by touching them with the tips of the fingers, which then tingle.

This effect, presumably, is generated by piezo-electricity, which is the power principle used in a quartz watch, where a small battery imparts a vibration to a quartz crystal. In the megaliths, the reverse effect occurs, caused by the considerable mechanical pressures acting upon the many quartz crystals inside the huge stone mass, due to the alternate heating and expansion of the stone in the warmth of the day, and its subsequent contraction in the cold of the night. This action within the stones causes the generation of electricity.

Furthermore, by dowsing, I have come to much the same conclusions as did Tom Lethbridge, Guy Underwood, and many others since their day, that the actual sites, together with the shape, form and meticulously careful positioning of the giant stones, generate energy which seems to ebb and flow at different times, and alters with different phases of the moon.

These energies can be picked up by people with sufficient sensitivity and can affect them, beneficially. In this sense, I believe that an identical effect can be felt by most people inside the massive stone-built Gothic cathedrals. Certainly, I have felt the power in them and in many other ancient churches, mosques and temples, where I have experienced a similar sensation, sending a current of electrical energy up my spine.

I am sure that many open-minded people also feel similar effects when visiting the ancient megaliths, that abound throughout Britain and Europe. Perhaps the whole reason for the existence of these impressive stone structures was best summed up, for me, by a conversation that I once overheard, regarding them.

One person asked another: 'Why were they built?'

The other replied, 'To affect the minds of men!'

By this I presume he also meant: the minds of women, and children, as well!

Whatever the reasons for their construction thousands of years ago, they should be preserved, at all costs, for they are very much a part of our heritage, which we must hand on to our children, together with a full, coherent explanation as to why we find them so important to our ecology and ethology.

Apart from the obvious places in our environment, like these megalithic structures, the Gothic cathedrals, old churches, mosques, synagogues, temples and many other buildings, both ancient and modern, that affect our lives how can we recognize other influential 'Places of the Heart'?

The answer lies in the abilities of the open-minded to sense the overall effect of any environment in which they find themselves.

As examples of some of these treasured spots on earth, let me summarize the sort of places that touch me, deeply.

I am very much a child of the chalk, having been brought up from early childhood in the environment of the long green dragons of the rolling North and South Downs, of Kent, Sussex and Surrey.

As a youngster, for eighteen years I drank the calcium-rich water and the milk from the downland cows. I ate the many products of the local, chalk-based soil, such as wheat, corn, and barley, and enjoyed the mutton and beef of the Romney Marsh and county farmlands, as well as the local vegetables and fruits, for which the counties of Kent and Sussex are famous. My brother also taught me to drink the full-flavoured local ales, which have been brewed there since Saxon times.

My bones are still strong, due to the calcium of that organic chalk, and my mind is full of happy memories of jewelled days, running through those broad downland meadows, enjoying the companionship of my beloved dogs, as we raced among the wind-stirred wavelets of grass, that rustled and flowed across the rolling landscape.

I am sure that most of my readers will have experienced something very similar to this sort of emotional appreciation of some part of their own land, or, for that matter, felt a love for parts of other countries, which have captured their imagination and affection.

When I first went to Peru, after the Second World War,

214

and met my father's Peruvian nurse, Angelica, that wonderful ninety-two-year-old lady, who still remembered him, always referred to the place where she was born, at Cerro de Pasco in the Sierra of the Andes, as '*Mi Tierra*' (My Land). Yet that marvellous lady had been brought down from her highlands, by my grandfather, when she was a child of seven and had never returned to her birthplace since that time. But Angelica still recalled the magic of that Place of the Heart, and it gave her immense pleasure to remember it.

Is this all just a convention, conjured up as some sort of a defence or pleasure mechanism, by the unconscious mind?

I don't think so, and neither do many of my dowser friends, for all of us can detect certain patterns, which seem to be generated by these special places in the environment.

When the Bloy brothers showed me how to dowse, I told them that I had experienced something of the sort before, especially when I was near some particular place, by the cold wave of awareness that used to sweep up my spine. I also told my new friends about my feelings for the rolling chalk downlands, and my beloved Romney Marsh, and the sensations of 'belonging' that certain parts of the earth aroused in me.

They told me of their own Places of the Heart, which gave them the same rippling chills up their backs. Then they explained to me that dowsing was all about 'searching and finding', especially for such places.

I have been fortunate enough to find a number of sites around the world that have the same wonderful effect on me. The Romney Marsh, flat and featureless, is only one of them. But when I sit on the escarpment above the levels, with those reedy dyke-cut water-meadows below me, I deeply sense the lie of that particular ancient land.

In spring, lambs gambol joyfully, or sleep beside their mothers in the lush grass, often beside a Saxon tumulus. In May, the guelder-roses, hawthorn, apple-blossom,

215

and flowering cherry-trees, shading the gardens of the scattered farm houses of the flat-lands, burst into bloom.

Suddenly, these water-meadows are full of colour as the rape crop blossoms into a yellow carpet, turning the marsh into an irregular chequer-board, of green and canary-coloured squares. Milk-white mist hovers over the sea-wall, hiding the sable sand of the beaches beyond.

The fury of the winter gales is forgotten in the crisp spring air. Yet, only weeks before, angry waves generated by the narrowing straits had thundered against the stone face of the sole barrier that keeps the marsh from drowning, the steely-grey waters sending towers of spray high into the air above the shuddering concrete glacis of the sea-wall.

At that bleak season, with snow-storms swirling across the Levels, this land is as bleak as Alaska, the white-out reducing visibility to a few yards, and even today it is a place of peril for a lost traveller.

But, when summer creeps over the marsh, bringing wild-fowl and sea-birds in their thousands, the shingle spread of Dungeness becomes a bird sanctuary and the breeding ground of the British gull.

The Levels turn into a place of sun-lit magic, drawing young and old to the seaside fringe with its lines of bungalows, holiday camps, and caravan sites, the children happily digging in the warm sands, or ecstatically paddling in the shallow waters of the gently shelving bay.

Thousands of families ride the fifteen-mile track of the New Romney Hythe and Dymchurch miniature railway; one of its eleven one third scale Steam Locomotives, with names like 'Doctor Syn' and 'Green Goddess', pulling long trains of carriages, filled with excited children, just as enthralled as I was, all those years ago when yesterday was young.

But few of the visitors venture inland, for those twisting roads and deep dykes can be dangerous, especially for children who do not know as we did the strange ways of the marshy Levels. Even at the height of the holiday season, the Romney Marsh can still be a solitary, peaceful place, especially in the pastel beauty of the autumn.

Then it is a Place of the Heart, for artists, writers, poets and lovers.

Walk over the length and breadth of those magical flatlands, holding a forked twig, dowsing rod or pendulum, and you will feel the life pulsing beneath the surface, as I do, and you will wonder at the intensity of its power.

That is why the Levels bring back people who can sense this energy, time after time, throughout their lives, eager once again to enjoy its magic.

Therefore, I believe that the quickest way for people to find these beneficial places, is to dowse for them, by whatever method best suits them, using their hands, as the antennae of their built-in, biological detection system.

Just as the Chinese Feng-Shui diviners sort out the flow and direction of the Lung-Mei, the dragon-lines of Yin and Yang, which archetypally cover the surface of the earth, so you can learn to locate your own most beneficial environment, by using similar methods. You don't have to make a deep study of this ancient Oriental art. Just allow yourself to open your mind to the existence of these forces, and accept the powerful effect that they have upon the collective unconscious mind, the universal overmind, human or otherwise.

Then you will begin to realize how much you, personally, can affect the course of your own life, as well as becoming aware of how many other manipulators of these extraneous forces, for their own purposes and profit, are trying to influence your mind.

I have found that Palm Springs, in California, is just such a Place of the Heart. I believe that this is because of the existence of the many lines of force, generated by the mineral-rich hot springs, lying deep under the lime-stone plain of its extensive desert environment.

These bubbling springs, which are part of the water table of the surrounding mountain ranges, seem to be

217

beneficial to the small community of artists and writers, who, like Professor Albert Einstein, found this place to be ideal for creative thinking.

This extraordinary desert area, which just a short time ago was a small, sleepy village, is rapidly growing into an extensive resort area surrounded by similar, satellite cities like Palm Desert, Rancho Mirage, Cathedral City, Desert Hot Springs, Indian Wells and other centres. People, many of them retired on slim pensions, have recognized in this great desert valley with its magnificent mountainous skyline, their Places of the Heart.

Inevitably, it won't be long before developers and exploiters will have ruined this beautiful environment, and then it will be time to move on, perhaps to some more remote desert place, like Borrego Springs, which is still almost untouched.

The North-American Indians, like those of the Agua Caliente, Morongo and Cahuilla tribes, still live in this area, as their ancestors have done, for centuries before them. Up till now, they were only allowed to *lease* their land to new settlers, but they are presently selling their terrain, which is their birthright, to persuasive developers.

These operators, being commercially motivated, immediately build large condominium complexes, with little or no regard for the environment, take their profits, and, invariably, go and live somewhere else.

My friend, Alan Grisè, an experienced physicist, gifted with an open mind and a sparkling wit, has shown me some fascinating experiments, connected with the lines of force, which criss-cross the Coachella valley. Having established, by dowsing, the existence of such a line, running north and south, Alan and I stood, facing each other, and carefully observed our respective, apparent heights. We then reversed our positions, once again facing each other.

To my surprise, our apparent heights had altered, even though the floor was level.

In the first instance, Alan, who is significantly taller than I am, appeared to be *much* taller, whereas, in the second instance, I seemed to be almost as tall as my friend.

When my wife, Clementina, who was most intrigued, watched the same experiment, she was surprised to observe this strange phenomenon, but from a different angle.

Later on in the winter, at Santa Cruz, near San Francisco, our son Richard, our late daughter Fusty (Marylla), Clementina and I, visited the famous 'Magnetic Anomaly', which is situated in a wood outside the town.

The owners of this strange place exploit its peculiar properties for commercial reasons, and, to that end, they have exaggerated the effects that the visitors to this site experience, by using structures which are set at a pronounced angle, to emphasize the illusion of these anomalies.

Life magazine published an article on the Santa Cruz phenomenon, and well over a million people have visited this strange place since its discovery, which I believe was in the early part of this century.

Even allowing for deliberate structural exaggeration of the effect of these anomalies, witnessed and observed by many valid and qualified researchers, nobody so far has come up with a satisfactory explanation for the phenomena, which would fit in with contemporary physics.

Put simply it does appear, according to my own experience and that of my family, that there exists in this small area of a few acres, with sharply defined parameters, a powerful force, possibly geo-magnetic, that distorts the local gravitational field, thereby causing extraordinary anomalies to become apparent.

I am not certain whether these phenomena, which range from objects apparently falling sideways, rather than downwards, or hanging at a pronounced angle to the perpendicular, are purely illusory, or whether they exist as actual physical phenomena.

But I *do* know that my legs responded, painfully, to the apparent increase in the localized gravitational field.

That definite strain on my calf-muscles, which, as a result of severe attacks of emboli over the years, causing acute phlebitis, have become sensitive to any increased pressure on my narrowed leg veins and arteries, was very pronounced, as I climbed a path, which seemed to slope upwards at only a slight angle, but which to my calf muscles felt like a *steep* climb.

The acute discomfort was unmistakable!

Once again, as with the experiment with Alan Grisè, the difference in respective heights became observable, apparent, and even photographically recordable. It was a fascinating experience.

What is all this leading up to?

To put it simply; I am convinced, beyond reasonable doubt, that Places of the Heart exist all over the earth, and that we humans, as a product and an integral part of this whole system, which we call the earth, can be affected by these energies to our great advantage, or evident harm, according to the type of force-field which is being generated by the environment.

From long experience, I know that these places affect me deeply, whether they are a vista, a familiar landscape, a sea-view, a skyline, a stone circle, a cathedral, a mosque, or a temple, a house, a garden, a room, or even just a favourite chair to sit in, at a *particular* spot.

For me, they are *all* treasured Places of the Heart.

If you have not already done so, I recommend that you seek out such places.

Assuredly, they will be among the greatest riches that you, your family, and, especially, your children will enjoy.

CHAPTER TEN

'You all know what to do, but I'll just go over it once more.'

That quotation is taken, verbatim, from a 'B' feature American science fiction film, where the director and scriptwriter were faced with the daunting task of having to explain to the cinema audience what the story was all about, at the final briefing to the movie *Astronauts*, before lift-off.

It also happens to sum-up what this chapter is about, because this is my final attempt to encapsulate the lessons I have learnt, and to try to pass them on to my readers.

First of all, I have no doubt that the pressures constantly being exerted on our minds, by unscrupulous manipulators, really do exist, and that only those with open minds are able to recognize and effectively resist this sort of psychic attack.

I am certain that the simple rules and exercises that my father taught me helped enormously to improve my chances in life, and I believe that they can be used to enlarge the personal horizons of those with imaginative minds, to greatly enhance and enrich their lives.

I am equally sure that the dangers that I have emphasized, are inherent in any quest, which takes the infranaut into the farthest reaches of the unconscious mind, and that the threat to the voyager's sanity can be averted by knowledge gained from experience.

Truth is one of the most important assets in our lives.

Happiness, based on ignorance, is at best, self-delusion, from which eventually the dreamer must wake and face the facts.

Nevertheless, I have found that continually dwelling on the thought of physical death is neither wise nor healthy and that all animals, while being well aware of their mortality, only face death when it becomes absolutely necessary. The rest of the time they simply get on with the process of survival.

It seems to me extraordinary how our attitudes, where death and sex are concerned, have altered in the period dating from the end of the nineteenth century to the last decades of this millennium.

In Victorian times, at any family gathering mourning garments were a common sight, mourning jewellery was often worn and people talked quite freely about death.

'I don't suppose Cousin Henry will last much longer.'

'Aunt Martha passed away, so peacefully, that one almost envies her.'

'Great-Uncle Bertie is about to meet his Maker.'

This complacent attitude towards mortality was prevalent throughout that whole era.

Yet if one word about sex crept into the general conversation, such as: 'Wasn't Aunt Martha in love with her music teacher, and didn't she become his mistress?' the reaction was swift and unequivocal.

'Leave the table, at once, Letitia! Go straight to your room and wash out your mouth with soap! I will not tolerate this sort of foul gossip at my dinner-table!'

Hypocrisy? Of course!

Today, the conversation goes something like this:

'Harriet is having it off with George and Mark. I wonder if they do it at the same time?'

'I hear that Harry is having ejaculation problems.'

'What! Again?'

'Martha has shacked up with Sybil. They're both into Gay Liberation, Zen and motor-bike maintenance. I don't know when they get the time to work.'

But if somebody makes a remark like: 'Hasn't poor old Johnny got AIDS?' immediately, the atmosphere darkens:

'Christ! Mavis. Not while we're eating!'

How things have changed!

However, attitudes to the paranormal haven't altered a great deal since Victorian times, when table-turning and seances were part of the social scene, ever since the famous Fox Sisters with their poltergeist type of phenomena caused such a stir, mid-century, at Hidesville in the United States.

Their paranormal phenomena consisted mainly of raps, sometimes so heavy that they shook the house. The physical mediums responsible for these manifestations were most probably the young sisters, who were little more than children when the phenomena started. They themselves were terrified at first, but later became accustomed to the loud physical manifestations that they seemed to generate everywhere.

In a vain attempt to 'expose' them, the establishment claimed that these heavy raps were caused by the sisters' *knee-joints cracking*, in the same way that people crack their knuckles!

When the Fox sisters finally became the centre of a detailed investigation, the researchers were generally in agreement over the genuineness of the phenomena. Their house became a centre of pilgrimage and they were largely responsible for the dramatic rise of Spiritualism in the United States.

At that time, the Church in its various forms had thundered forth, roundly condemning them in terms of Devil Worship, Spiritism, as Spiritualism was then called, and other 'Satanic' practices.

Yet, conversely, clever men, like Sir Oliver Lodge, Lord Kelvin, Sir William Crookes, Karl Von Reichenbach, Sir Arthur Conan Doyle, *et al*, and equally talented women, such as Anna Petrovna Blavatsky, Annie Besant, and the mourning Queen Victoria had opened their minds to forces, other than those of the ultra-materialistic society in which they lived.

For example, the remarkable mediumship of Daniel

Dunglass Home was probably the most outstanding, and it is interesting that this Scottish-born, American psychic did *not* take money for his seances. His physical mediumship covered the whole range of paranormal powers, from remarkable clairvoyance and prophecy to complete levitation, in which he once floated out of a room *through a third-floor window* and back again.

His extraordinary mediumship is fully described by Colin Wilson, in his excellent book, *The Occult*, which is well worth reading for a balanced overview of the paranormal.

At about the same time, Maria Silbert, in Austria, had produced quite outstanding results with her physical mediumship. Among other phenomena, she produced full materializations in her garden *in broad daylight*. These manifestations were witnessed by several observers, with impeccable credentials.

The practice of ritual-magic also flourished, in the nineteenth century, in the hands of such adepts as Lord Lytton, Eliphas Levi (a French magician, whose real name was Louis Constant), William Barratt, and the small group of British Gnostics who called their Order: 'The Golden Dawn'.

Meanwhile, the Society for Psychical Research, a respectable scientific body of interested and objective researchers, was set up, in 1882, in London under the guidance of Sir William Barrett, a noted physicist (not to be confused with William Barratt, who wrote: *The Magus*, an early nineteenth-century book on ritual-magic), and embarked on its long career. Today it is still flourishing, and is at present located in Adam Mews, just off Baker Street.

In this latter part of the twentieth century, genuine researchers can enjoy the advantages of the excellent Harry Price Library, at London University. This unique bequest is named after the noted psychic researcher of the twenties and thirties, who also bequeathed his collection of rare books on this subject, as well as much fascinating memorabilia, including hundreds of photographs of his many psychic investigations. It is well worth a visit.

Since 1946, we have seen a renewed interest in the study of paranormal phenomena, which lapsed during the Second World War.

This resurgence of investigation beyond the frontiers of conventional science was largely due to the work of Doctor Rhine, at Duke University, Carolina. It is because of him that we now use the word 'Parapsychology' to describe the modern study of the paranormal. Doctor Rhine also coined the words 'Psi factor' to describe: a sensitive person's paranormal abilities.

Recently, we have had the inauguration of a Chair of Parapsychology at Edinburgh University, the result of the controversial bequest by the late Arthur Koestler, the well-known Austrian-born author and political correspondent, who was a close friend of Carl Jung, and whose experiences, as a young journalist, imprisoned during the Spanish Civil War, first brought him international recognition. His excellent books on the paranormal, such as *The Janus Effect*, make compulsive reading.

The list of highly-qualified researchers into these areas of human behaviour is extensive and impressive. Therefore, it seems strange that, only a few years ago, a number of scientists, some 170 in all, banded together and swore a Solemn Oath, whatever that means, to expose all the quackery and pseudo-science that masquerades under the cloak of parapsychology!

This somewhat melodramatic proclamation sounds more like a Papal Bull of the Middle Ages than a scientific pronouncement!

As to why these technologists should be so vehemently outspoken is a debatable point, but their *unscientific* outburst is hardly commensurate with the serious research recently undertaken at Berkeley and Stanford Universities by such highly-qualified scientists as Professor William Tiller, and Doctors Harry Puthoff and Russell Targ.

The Pentagon has taken a great deal of interest in their experiments with mental telepathy and remote-viewing. Meanwhile, at Birkbeck College in London, Professor John Hastead has carried out extensive work on telekinesis, in the form of many well-observed experiments in metal-bending by the use of mental power, mainly conducted with children, with fascinating results.

Besides which, a number of other universities, world-wide, have founded chairs of parapsychology. In addition to this, it is hardly a secret that both the Soviet Academy of Science and the Pentagon have funded special departments to deal with all aspects of paranormal phenomena.

Consequently, the action of those 170 or so scientists and technologists condemning *all* contemporary research into the paranormal seems to be a peculiarly retrograde step.

Once an interested reader starts to examine the ramifications of this field of human and animal behaviour and its effect on our lives, he, or she, will be astounded at the enormous amount of serious, well-documented evidence that there is, freely available, in support of the validity of the world-wide range of paranormal experience.

However, a difficulty soon becomes evident.

Which particular works on the vast field of the paranormal should be consulted, to form a firm base for further study?

In view of the vast amount of well-researched evidential material available to the student of the paranormal, why then is there still such vehement resistance, by the closed-minded brigade, against the study of this field of human behaviour?

Obviously, ignorance, and therefore fear, plays a key role in such bigoted condemnation of all research into this field.

Furthermore, this sort of drastic reaction is not unusual when any Establishment is faced with heresy that threatens its complacent security, as the spokespersons for the system that it claims to represent.

This attitude of mind is probably an overspill from the constant attacks over the centuries by many of the established churches, who once held enormous temporal power over most of the people of the world. Since then, a number of world churches have lost much of their credence, probably by reason of the appalling loss of life and the dreadful suffering caused by two devastating global wars, which they, as the self-proclaimed representatives of God on earth, seemed powerless to prevent, or even significantly influence.

The tremendous wave of atheism that swept through Russia helped to create the Soviet Union and the world Communist revolution. In fact, it made idols of Marx and Lenin. This was due, largely, to the Russian Orthodox Church's failure to bring peace and happiness to the hundreds of millions of devout worshippers, despite the religious Establishment's colossal wealth, amid the stark contrast of the dire poverty of most of the believers.

Today, the same violent reaction of resentment and bitter hatred against the wealth and former power of the Churches, in the form of terrorism, is being felt throughout South America, Africa, Asia and many other parts of the world. It is not just coincidence, that the prime targets of extremists and revolutionary fanatics are often priests and nuns, many of these tragic victims of torture and rape being dedicated and selfless people, who have done their tireless best for their poverty-stricken parishioners.

During the Russian Revolution, the Spanish Civil War, the obscenity of the Third Reich, the Stalinist purges, the Red Guards' Revolution in China, and amid various bloody military coups, in Africa, Asia and South America, it was often the priests and nuns of the various established churches, who were butchered.

Why?

I believe that loss of faith, or complete lack of faith, can be a terrible thing, and that the subsequent rage and despair at the horror of the vacuum that is left (the 'Horror Vacuo', of Freudian psychology) can turn very quickly to violence, especially against those who represent religion, and a spiritual alternative to the emptiness and the loneliness of dialectic materialism.

This unappeased hunger for spiritual comfort seems to be the reason why millions of Americans, of every race, creed and ethnic background, are now turning to the hyped-up image of the television fundamentalists, with their Bible-thumping rhetoric, currently being broadcast over that hypnotic medium. These television ministries have recently been under fire, because of the sexual and financial indiscretions of some of the revivalist preachers.

I watched one of these hellfire-and-damnation orators 'confessing', through floods of tears, his 'Fall from Grace'. It was a bravura performance, which just missed being pure ham. The hysterical audience, for that is what it seemed to me to be rather than a congregation, was entranced. Men and women moaned and groaned in chorus with the sobbing preacher, amid cries of 'Hallelujah!' and 'Praise the Lord.'

There was no denying the absolute sincerity of the people present at this bizarre exhibition, but being in show business I sensed that there were also a few 'plants' among the congregation, helping to set the overall hysterical pace.

The television director kept cutting to the more emotionally-disturbed members of the public, to emphasize the posturing preacher's melodramatic pleas for forgiveness.

It was yet another disturbing demonstration of television's .aptitude for mind manipulation, and a nasty reminder of how similar to the effective methods employed by the Nazis at their pre-war Nuremberg Rallies some of those techniques used at fundamentalist meetings can be.

The people in these devout congregations are swept along by the rousing rhetoric of the scripture-quoting spellbinders, who often prance about flourishing their

Bibles, as they overemphasize each preposition, adjective and adverb, in order to make their point.

It is a scene reminiscent of those archetypal movie courtroom dramas, where the defending counsel runs the whole gamut of emotions and then is accused by the prosecuting attorney of: 'Trying to influence the jury by the use of cheap histrionics.'

This television fundamentalism is very much a part of the contemporary American scene, which often seems so alien to the British sense of understatement, and it certainly works for millions of Americans who are seeking something they desperately need, beyond the purely materialistic benefits of their capitalist society.

There is no doubt about that!

Furthermore, the born-again Christians back up their faith with money, which they often can ill afford, to give to these ministries, for a great number of these devout worshippers are retired folk living just above the poverty line on fragile pensions.

For these needy people in both the material and spiritual sense, to have their faith suddenly and so rudely shaken, must be a tragic experience, shattering whatever peace and contentment they may have gained from their Church.

It says much for their courage and good-nature that in, at least, two cases of these unmasked 'Whited Sepulchres', as the rival Bible-thumping preachers referred to their 'fallen' colleagues, the fundamentalist congregations have forgiven the 'sinners' by an overwhelming majority.

Religion, hyped by extensive television and radio coverage, is very big business in the United States, bringing in billions of dollars, overall, in the form of donations from their 'Pray-a-thons', those twelve to twenty-four hour duration broadcast drives for financial support.

The Elders of each of these ministries certainly wield enormous power behind the scenes, while the front-men and women, the preachers themselves, often enjoy lifestyles that movie stars might well envy. One preacher's salary was estimated at well over a million dollars annually, plus perks, and even then that particular fundamentalist church was trying to get this huge sum, *tax-free*, as the organization is, arguably, a registered charity!

Such extremism in religion is very much part of the American Way of life and it was only a few years ago in Guiana that the Reverend Jones, an American preacher of mesmeric power, led over nine hundred members of his flock to their deaths by poison. Many of the victims were children. It was a dreadful indictment of deliberately *induced* religious mania.

Whichever way you look at it, modern media-hyped religion in America, is an amazing fact of life! If misused, it can have terrifying consequences.

More than ever before I can see how important it is to retain a healthy sense of humour and proportion when investigating these areas of paranormal behaviour, and I realize what a valuable contribution my cheerful mother made to keeping the balance, when, as a family, we were researching this form of human experience.

Commonsense is still one of our greatest aids to survival.

My own experience of involuntary clairvoyance with a definitive predictive content, giving me a quick and accurate glimpse of the *probable* future, has been of incalculable help in times of crisis, or at certain crossroads in my life. For me, it has been a vitally important part of my survival mechanism.

However, these unexpected flashes of intuitive insight are not always connected with a future occurrence. They also can be a detailed *overview* of a past event. For example, I looked through just such a 'window' on the past while visiting a close friend in southern Spain. This was the late Madeleine Carroll, that beautiful actress of the thirties and forties.

Highly intelligent, with an irrepressible sense of humour, Madeleine became a dear friend almost from the moment we met, many years ago while I was writing in that part of Europe. Deeply conscious of the spiritual side of life, this delightful Irish woman, whose mother had been French, was well aware of the power of her intuition which she possessed in abundance.

While listening to Madeleine speaking of a close friend of hers, Antoine Saint Exupery, the famous airman, poet and author, who had been one of my heroes when I was boy, I suddenly *subjectively* saw exactly how he had been killed in an air-crash, during the latter part of the war.

I saw Saint X, as Madeleine always referred to him, flying in an American P38, twin-engined fighter plane, low over water. I also sensed that this was close inshore to the coast of the south of France. As the plane banked low over the sea, a powerful gust of wind sweeping down from the mountains above Menton seemed to catch the aircraft in an unbalanced moment and tipped the wing, so that the airplane cartwheeled into the Mediterranean, instantly killing the famous pilot.

Madeleine, who had served with the Red Cross in Italy at that time, was fascinated by my description, but she told me that, according to the US Air Force report of his death, Saint X was believed to have been shot down by German fighters while on a reconnaissance mission.

Six weeks later, an excited Madeleine rang me up and invited me to dinner at her villa in the foothills of the mountains above San Pedro de Alcantara. She would not tell me why, but she said that I would be very interested in some news that she had just received.

After dinner, she showed me an article that had appeared in a current French magazine written by a woman journalist, who had been fascinated by Saint Exupery's life.

The article emphasized that the French pilot had not been shot down by the Germans, but had been the victim of a *freak accident*, while low-flying, on reconnaissance over the sea, close to the coast of the South of France.

As his group of twin-engined P38 fighter planes was based near Foggia, in northern Italy, this could have been well within the area of his assignment.

The writer of the article went on to quote from an eye-witness, whom she had traced and who had seen the actual off-shore crash of just such an Allied plane. Checking back as far as dates and times were concerned, the journalist had then confirmed the eye-witness report with the known facts according to US Air Force sources.

She also had ascertained that no other flight by an aircraft of that type had taken place in that specific area, on that particular day.

The words that the writer had quoted from the eye-witness's description of the tragedy exactly described what I had seen, clairvoyantly, some six weeks before the article was published.

Madeleine then told me that she was now convinced that I had witnessed the events leading to Saint X's death, because his family owned a villa in that part of the world and that, in all probability, the famous flyer was using his mission to make an unofficial sentimental journey to a Place of the Heart.

She also asked me how I had been so certain that what I had seen had been the actual circumstances of her beloved friend's death.

I involuntarily replied: 'I think Saint X told me so!'

'Yes', said Madeleine, with that wonderful smile of hers. 'I'm sure you're right!'

She told me of the many times her intuition had come to her aid, especially in times of crisis, and how much she had come to rely on this sixth sense, as Madeleine referred to it, using a term popular in the thirties.

We often talked about the paranormal, in conversations enriched with her perceptive sense of humour as she looked so deeply into life and saw the funny side of it, with wit, clarity and compassion. This remarkable woman, who was one of the great beauties of her era, had a gold aura which glowed round her, especially when she spoke of the past.

Somehow, I had been fortunate enough to turn the key to Madeleine's door of remembrance and, to my surprise, this very private person revealed to me many of her extraordinary experiences. I would never break that confidence, and her remarkable life-story once more confirmed, for me, the enormous importance of following one's intuition, along the pathway to destiny.

One question which is often asked me is: 'Have you ever seen a ghost?'

I usually reply: 'What sort of ghost are you referring to?'

For example, five years ago, I was a guest at a dinner given by the Red Arrows, the Royal Air Force's famous aerobatic team, at their base at Scampton, the wartime airfield, from which 617 Squadron, portrayed in *The Dam-Busters* film, had operated.

I knew it well from those dreadful months, during the long winter of 1943-44, when we had been at the height of the RAF bomber operations against the Third Reich and suffered such terrible casualties.

It was a hilarious evening and the atmosphere in the Mess recalled vivid flashes of memory, which were initiated for me by the Lancaster Mark 3 bomber which stood inside the gates, as a memorial to all our comrades who did not return from those raids.

After dinner the young adjutant, a tall, bespectacled, flight-lieutenant, approached me and asked if he could have a word, in private.

A chill rippled up my spine, indicating that he was going to relate a paranormal experience.

I was not disappointed.

'Something has been worrying me,' he said, diffidently. 'Some weeks ago, I was doing my rounds, as orderly officer, accompanied by the orderly sergeant, and part of our duties was to check that all buildings on the airfield were secure. It was one of those cold nights, with a full moon, that we often get here in Lincolnshire.'

I nodded, for I remembered them well.

'As we approached the site of the old 'Ops' buildings, of which the wartime control-tower still stands just as it did forty years ago, the full moon shone out brightly from behind the scattered clouds. The orderly sergeant went towards one side of the building and I approached the other side of the watchtower, facing the runway.'

He paused, awkwardly, as though he was embarrassed at what he was going to say, next.

'Go on,' I encouraged him. 'I'm listening, and I think I know what you are going to tell me.'

Then it all came out in a rush. 'I saw an airman, in full Second World War flying-kit, appear round the corner of the old control tower and walk towards me. He was carrying a large canvas hold-all and had on a chest-type parachute harness, over an orange lifejacket, but without the parachute pack attached. I saw him, as clearly as I see you now. He was solid, but I am sure that he was a ghost.'

'And did the orderly sergeant see the phantom airman as well?'

'I called out to him, as the ghost came towards me, and my sergeant hurried back. I'm sure he caught a glimpse of the apparition. But by the time he reached me, the ghost had vanished. What was it all about, sir? Have I gone potty?'

My age and white hair rather than my wartime rank had elicited his mark of respect, but obviously he trusted me and I felt certain that he was telling me the truth.

A similar ghost story had happened to me in 1943, at Wickenby, a wartime bomber airfield which was only a short distance up the road from Scampton airfield.

'In the winter of '43–'44, we used to call such moonlit nights "Bomber's Moon", and it is most likely that an operation would have been laid on under those conditions.

234

'What you saw was, probably, a replay of an actual event, rather like a television recording, but four-dimensional, locked in time in the vicinity of the wartime tower and the old "Ops" building, and released by the duplication of the moonlit circumstances.

'If you consider the building itself as a matrix of materials, containing significant amounts of quartz and silica, you are looking at a large complex of solid circuitry, rather like a giant video-recorder.

'You are evidently a sensitive person and I believe that you picked up the four-dimensional "recording" of a dramatic wartime event. After all, we are electro-chemical beings and our strongest emotions such as tension, fear and excitement as well as happiness or sorrow are also electrical phenomena and can impress their characteristics, at the moment of their occurrence, on the solid-circuitry around them such as that wartime watchtower.

'Similar apparitions are not unknown, especially in the vicinity of old battlefields, and on wartime aero-dromes.'

The young RAF officer visibly relaxed.

'I knew you would listen to me, because I've heard you talk about this sort of thing, on radio.'

Then I told him how, in the winter of 1943, on returning from leave at around midnight, I had seen the ghost of a good friend, flight-lieutenant 'Pop' Walker, whose large and distinctive appearance was unmistakable in the bright mid-winter moonlight, walk past me without speaking in the direction of his Nissen hut.

I had waved to him as I entered my own quarters in a nearby Nissen hut, which I shared with five other young officers.

My comrades, who were all aircrew, were sound asleep, so I had taken care not to waken them.

In the early morning our batman, a cheerful cockney, had brought us our mugs of tea and shaving water. He commiserated with me on the loss of my friend, F/Lt

Walker, in a crash two nights before, when I had been on leave.

Ice-cold with shock, I stammered: 'How can he be dead? I saw him when I got back, late last night!'

Our batman and the others looked at me, as if I had gone mad.

'That's impossible, sir,' said the cockney. 'Mister Walker was killed hours before that!'

The sense of extreme cold should have warned me on that occasion, but, after all, the winter's night had been icy, and I had no inkling whatsoever that my friend had been killed.

I am sure that the flight-lieutenant adjutant, at Scampton, like myself, at my wartime airfield at Wickenby, a few miles up the road, had undergone a paranormal experience, and we both regretted that we had not tried to speak to our respective ghosts.

Quite another type of apparition manifested frighteningly to an American journalist friend of mine, Bob Rooney. This open-minded and witty Irish-American pressman has seen and done most things, but up to the time of his paranormal experience, he had been sceptical of ghosts, ghoulies and things that went bump in the night.

As he said: it came as a terrific shock when the paranormal finally caught up with him. Even more surprising was where and when the phenomenon had occurred.

Rooney was in London, job-hunting for work as a movie-publicist and had been introduced to a top film production company in Wardour Street, where there was every opportunity for the employment of his talents. It looked like nothing could go wrong.

Being an accomplished professional, my friend was confident and relaxed on that winter's morning in the early sixties. The last thing he expected was that, within minutes of his arrival at these imposing offices, he would be involved in a terrifying paranormal experience.

Everything was proceeding splendidly, when the door to an inner office opened and a grey-haired man in shirt sleeves entered the room and spoke to the executive, who was interviewing Rooney:

'Can I have a word with you, in private?' he said.

'Sure,' replied the executive, and excused himself, as the two men went into the other office and closed the door.

The other two people present looked at my friend in astonishment, for the American journalist's face, suddenly, had turned grey with shock and he was shaking uncontrollably.

'What's the matter, Rooney? You look like you've just seen a ghost!'

'I-I-I. . . h. . . have!' My friend stuttered, his eyes bulging in terror and his trembling finger pointing at the door of the inner office.

'Who the hell is that man?' he asked, his face running with the cold sweat of fear.

One of them mentioned the name of a famous Hollywood producer. Rooney dropped into a chair and tried to calm his nerves. He knew for certain that he had just blown an excellent opportunity of getting the job. He was badly shaken and Bob was too honest a man to keep his mouth shut.

'I gotta tell you,' he said, in a quavering voice. 'That guy had a *Demon*, right behind him. I saw it, as plainly as I see you now.

'Its face was horrifying, green and scaly, with long red eyes burning in its head, and its mouth was twisted in an evil grin, showing its fangs. It was the most scary thing I ever saw.'

Absolute silence had fallen in that ultra-modern production office, as the others stared at Rooney, in shocked disbelief.

237

'What's more,' he continued, knowing that his last chance of a job with the company had gone. 'That damned thing leered at me and winked, as though to say: I'm not after you. I'm with him. This man is mine!'

Rooney is one of the most reliable friends I know, and a professional journalist of the highest calibre and integrity.

I unreservedly accept his story, which, normally, he is reluctant to tell. In fact he will only relate it to a sympathetic listener.

I know only too well how such valid paranormal experiences usually are received.

The sequel to Bob Rooney's terrifying experience is interesting.

The very expensive film that the grey-haired man was engaged in producing ran into difficulties that few movies have ever known, costing millions over budget.

It was also a box-office failure, because it couldn't recoup its huge production costs, though it made a new international star out of one of its top players, Richard Burton.

The name of the film was *Cleopatra*.

It certainly brought little happiness to its stars, Richard Burton and Elizabeth Taylor, who married and divorced, remarried and then finally parted. Moreover, since *Cleopatra*, neither of those two nice people's lives could be said to have been particularly happy.

Nor could that of the producer, Walter Wanger, a brilliant, imaginative man, who made many famous films. He seemed to have been dogged by inexplicable misfortune, and he had become a tragic figure, when he was arrested and charged with shooting the alleged lover of his wife, Joan Bennett.

Considering Bob Rooney's terrifying experience of, unexpectedly, seeing that evil over-shadowing presence behind him, I feel that here was a case of a good man, in desperate need of help.

238

I also believe that what Rooney sensed, in his own words: 'With my inner vision', i.e. *subjectively*, was a symbolic indication that this unfortunate man was about to be involved in a series of further misfortunes, and, to Bob's mind, trained as a Catholic, this manifested as the presence of a demonic force.

Britain, being a land wrapped in mystery and cloaked in the long mantle of its turbulent history, has many '4-D recordings' of past events, most of which were extremely violent and therefore heavily charged with tension. These are inclined to be replayed, whenever certain circumstances are duplicated, and wherever a person with enough sensitivity and an open mind is present to witness the event.

For example, there are other airfields like Scampton, including one near Sunderland, that I have dowsed, where I detected a strong line of force in an area inside the hangar, where I was told later that paranormal phenomena has been observed. In that case it was the apparition of a young First World War airman, a pilot killed in an aircrash, who has been seen many times since his death.

Apparently, he is very angry, which is understandable in the circumstances.

Perhaps, a 'Rescue' circle, such as the ones that my father, Eddie Partridge and others of Pop's colleagues held in the thirties, might help to break the cycle of this particular apparition. During those pre-war sittings, a number of distraught and confused discarnate entities appeared to manifest. Apparently my father's team helped them to understand their pitiable plight of being unaware that they were dead, thereby releasing them from the repeated cycle of their last memory of life on earth.

This type of seance might assist such an angry and deeply-disturbed spirit, such as the ghost of the dead pilot, to gain understanding of his sad circumstances and gain his subsequent release.

In the Sunderland case, I believe that we would be dealing with an entity who is locked in time by the violence of his accidental death, rather than with a recorded event of a general nature, such as the appearance of the aircrew member seen by the young adjutant at Scampton. That is why I regret not having *immediately* recognized that 'Pop' Walker was a ghost and failed to speak to him.

As we were good friends and had discussed aspects of the supernatural, as it was known at that time, it is possible that he appeared to me shortly after his death with some purpose in mind. In which case I failed him, if indeed his intent was to communicate with me, perhaps with the idea of my writing about my experience to his widow and children as an indication of his survival.

I still feel that I should have been aware that my friend had been killed – but – perhaps I was just too tired to pick this up.

Having gone through a facsimile of the death-change myself on two occasions, I can understand how confusing such an experience could be, if the mind of the person undergoing it was firmly closed or very materialistic in character.

It must be like an unending nightmare.

However, in 'Pop' Walker's case his mind was an open one and his warmth, kindness and commonsense are still a treasured memory.

Although my friend had safely completed his tour of operations with this particular bomber wing, he had volunteered to accompany a new, 'Sprog', crew on that fatal night and had been killed by a combination of the inexperience of the young pilot and bad weather, which had hidden the hilly wolds in cloud, causing the aircraft to crash.

Alternatively, as I have explained, it may be that the illusion of a ghost is often the replaying of events leading up to tragedy, that were impressed on the solid-circuitry of a building, or on a specific area, such as a battlefield.

An RAF dog-handler, who trained Alsatian and German Shepherd guard-dogs, once told me that his animals would never cross such places, no matter how hard he tried to make them do so.

'I think they sense the blood which has been spilled there,' he said.

I believe him!

After all, we know so little about our own circumstances of life and death, that we are not really in a position of omniscience to evaluate much of this type of phenomena.

I have known so many sensible people during my own lifetime who have had parallel experiences, that I am completely open-minded about such things. Moreover, whenever I write about these matters and appear on television or talk on radio about this subject, I receive a large number of letters relating equally puzzling experiences which many people have undergone.

Many of these letters ask for help and assistance, often in easing great pain and grief for the loss of some well-loved person, and many of them wring the heart, with their feeling of sadness. My wife and I try to help, but even if we worked full-time on such a task we would soon be overwhelmed by its magnitude.

This is where I feel that the church frequently has failed to fulfil its true mission. Surely, this is one of religion's *raisons d'être*: to help those who are wracked with the agony of grief.

I would like to see healing sessions included in *every* church service, containing prayers for the healing and guidance of our country, and the rest of the world in its present confused state of divisiveness.

It seems to me that a liberal democratic society, based on unselfish commonsense and full of compassion is one thing, and a social system based on all-embracing permissiveness and widespread bureaucracy is something quite different.

241

In essence, permissiveness is more like the: 'Do what thou wilt shall be the whole of the Law' philosophy of Aleister Crowley, and soon leads to disaster.

My friend Colin Bloy, who is a manufacturer of printing-ink, started an interesting series of experiments with a prayer group, called 'The Fountain Group', after the stone fountain situated outside one of Brighton's oldest churches in the centre of that town. These experiments were conducted for the specific purpose of trying to regain our present troubled society's lost equilibrium, which had become particularly evident in Brighton.

Deeply disturbed by the mindless violence and crime that was holding this lovely seaside town on Britain's south coast in an ever-tightening grip of fear, a number of local citizens of goodwill decided to do something about the insupportable situation.

With the help of a local priest they invited a number of local leaders of the different religious communities who reside in Brighton, to meet at this church and band themselves together into a small non-denominational task-force, with the object of linking-up at agreed times to form a prayer-circle of positive thinking, similar to the contemplative Orders of many established churches.

The prayers took place in the members' own homes, at a specific time in the evening after work, each one of them linking his, or her, mind with those of the other members of the group, who were also sitting quietly in their own houses.

No matter of what religion, race, creed, or colour, the members of the Fountain Group might be, the object of their prayers was the same: To ask, through positive thought, for peace and goodwill to return to the town and for this ambience to be sustained within its environment.

The results were impressive, and according to the police in subsequent conversations with Colin and others of the group, violence, hooliganism, and other serious crimes, involving grievous bodily harm, showed a marked reduction.

Coincidental? Perhaps!

But the results were so encouraging that other Fountain Groups have been established in Britain, as well as in many other parts of the world, with similar results in varying degrees, whenever and wherever the participants went about this simple procedure of positive prayer, using their commonsense and sincerity in an orderly manner.

In other words, these groups generate cosmos: mental and spiritual order.

Once again, we were seeing the same sort of result on a much smaller scale of the extraordinary effectiveness of those wartime 'Days of National Prayer', which Winston Churchill had initiated in 1940, and which were celebrated by ordinary people of goodwill, no matter what their religion, everywhere in war-torn Britain.

In the final analysis, the Nazis were defeated by the unified positive thinking and self-sacrifice of ordinary men and women, dedicated to their task; a perfect example of the positive power of the 'group-mind'.

Why not try the same sort of ecumenical spiritual approach to the problems of violent crime and hooliganism in your town or city?

I find the practice of protection against different forms of evil to be both valid and effective. I hope I have established the fact that evil exists, as a state of mind in all of us, to a greater or lesser extent according to how soon we recognize its presence and start to neutralize its effects.

One experience I witnessed of a psychic attack, psychological or otherwise, by a group of Satanists, was against an intelligent elderly woman and it is worth recounting, because I was involved with helping her to endure the mental anguish that she was suffering.

I had been asked to help Miss F by a mutual friend, who had known her since the days when both of them had been members of clandestine wartime organizations, in the Special Operations Executive.

Miss F, an expert calligrapher, had then been engaged

in producing forged documents for our field agents and operatives in Europe. After the war she had returned to the practice of calligraphy, and had become an acknowledged authority on that fascinating craft.

The lady herself was tall and slim, with fine-boned features indicative of a keen intellect and a strong will. There was no sense of weakness in Miss F's face. Yet, when we met at a private dedication of a plaque in memory of a number of our gallant female operatives who had been murdered by the Nazis, I sensed that this formidable woman was terrified of something.

Our mutual friend introduced us and straightaway she asked me for help, telling me that she believed herself to be under intensive psychic attack.

I believed her, because of her air of acute distress which, though tightly controlled, was evident to anyone who was sensitive to the kind of chilling atmosphere that accompanies an assault of this sort.

Clementina, my wife, also found her to be deeply disturbing, but was willing to help someone who was so evidently desperate. Then and there we agreed to drive Miss F back to her London home and to listen to her story. She owned a small cottage in a mews, which was set back from the main road, in Marylebone. As the lady had been part of what British wartime Intelligence had called 'The Baker Street Irregulars', after Conan Doyle's immortal description of Holmes and Watson, her London *pied-à-terre* seemed to be appropriately sited.

On the outside this mews cottage was a cheerful white-painted example of its genre, and the same bright decor had been carried out inside the place. But even with this light-filled colour scheme there was no mistaking the intense cold that permeated the atmosphere, and though that spring morning was warm and sunny, my wife and I both shivered in the alchemical chill that seemed to pervade the whole cottage.

It was like walking into the ice-cold atmosphere of a mortuary.

244

I sensed that Clementina much regretted her decision to accompany Miss F to her mews home and that she wanted to leave as soon as possible.

Miss F was adamant and I felt constrained to listen to her vivid description of the psychic attack, which she believed was being aimed against her.

She came straight to the point.

'I understand that you are a trained psychic and that you can help me. I have fallen foul of a powerful Satanic coven, which is situated in the Home Counties, near my house by the river. I came under their concentrated attack while helping a close friend, who had become deeply involved with this circle of ritual-magicians, who practise Black Magic!

'Please tell me frankly: Can you help me?'

I was reluctant to give an immediate decision, especially as Clementina was becoming more apprehensive by the minute. However, I felt I had to do something.

'I am not a ritualist, nor am I qualified to take on a task such as you describe. But I have some knowledge of these matters and can put you in touch with people who can help you.'

Miss F heaved an audible sigh of relief and, for the first time since we had met on that bright spring morning, her eyes lost the haunted look that had so bothered Clementina and myself.

'What have you done so far?' I asked.

Without another word, Miss F took me into her bedroom and opened a white-painted cupboard.

Inside, neatly laid out on sheets of black paper were small individual photographs of several men and women, each one stuck to a piece of white card and enclosed in series of closely-drawn concentric circles, seven in number. Near them was a compass.

I recognized this as a ritual-magician's symbolic defence.

'Are you, yourself, a practising magician?' I asked bluntly, for the lady had inferred previously that it was her friend who had become involved with the ritual coven.

'No. I am a dowser! That is a dowser's defence.'

At that time I was studying dowsing with the Bloy brothers and others and I felt that Miss F was not telling me the whole truth. I wanted to leave then and there, but the lady's plight was so desperate that I decided to stay a little longer, to pass on to her the names and addresses of those more qualified than I was to deal with this type of evil.

All the time I felt energy being drawn from me, and I could see that Clementina was trying to stifle her yawns, a sure sign to me that our vital force was being tapped. In view of the victim's desperate need for strength, I could sympathize with her motive, but I could not allow that sort of psychic 'vampirism' to continue.

I told her that we had to leave and passed on the appropriate information, as quickly as I could. Miss F was very reluctant to let us go, but I could now feel the situation was getting out of hand and that we were being deliberately used by a desperate woman, who was near the end of her powers of resistance. However, I was adamant and we left.

It must have been around one o'clock in the afternoon of that fine spring day, when we set off back for our home in Surrey.

'She frightens me,' said Clementina, with a shiver. 'I don't like the whole thing. That cottage was like a grave. It was bitterly cold and it reeked of fear!'

I agreed with her, but I was committed morally to help this wartime colleague, especially as I had been asked to do so by our mutual friend, an ex-Intelligence officer from our wartime Dutch section.

Quite suddenly as we sped home I felt overwhelmingly tired, almost as though I had been drained completely of all my vital energy. Without consciously doing so I slowed down the car and pulled it into the side of the Kingston bypass, realizing with alarm that, at that same moment, I had actually been about *to fall asleep at the wheel*.

When you consider that this was happening in the middle of a bright, crisp spring day, and that neither Clementina nor I had taken a drink, other than our breakfast coffee, that overpowering sense of fatigue seemed to me to be no accident. But it had certainly nearly caused one, for we had been driving along the busy bypass at the regulation speed of seventy miles an hour, when that frightening wave of exhaustion had so nearly overcome me.

Subsequently, Miss F was helped by my various friends, who were psychics and scholars, but she had a close brush with the power of evil, and before the psychic attack was over she had fallen heavily and had been severely hurt.

For her it must have been a terrifying experience.

Was it all coincidence?

I doubt it because of that inexplicable feeling of total fatigue and the sense of extreme cold that both Clementina and I had felt in her brightly painted mews cottage, and which was so unexpected on that sunny day.

In view of her information about the existence of a powerful coven of Satanists, on the lines of Stephen Ward's group at Cliveden, and, presumably, their probable use of drugs as well, I mentioned this to my friends in Special Branch, and at Scotland Yard.

Their reaction was interesting.

They made enquiries, in the area that Miss F had designated as the site of the coven's operations and, sure enough, there was a suspected ritual magical group of wealthy people practising in that region.

But being a Satanist is not in itself a felony in our country and unless such a coven has committed an actual crime, within the meaning of the criminal code of law, the authorities are powerless to move against them. Therefore although they were believed to be actively involved in the practice of Satanism their existence as a

247

practising ritual group did not constitute sufficient reason for interference with their activities, unless they *overtly* broke the law.

Miss F herself was also known to the authorities in the area, as she had gone to them for help on behalf of her friend. They even had some doubts about her sanity, in view of the extraordinary accusations that she had made. Had I not known her past case-history, which our mutual Dutch friend had given me, and had I not suffered that extraordinary onset of sudden exhaustion while driving home, I might well have felt the same way about Miss F.

However, Clementina and I had both undergone such an unpleasant reaction from the circumstances surrounding our meeting with the lady, that I accepted her validity and, in view of the confirmation of the existence of a practising Satanic coven in that area, the logical explanation seemed that her story was true.

Be that as it may, it took a great deal of effort and concentration on the part of my various colleagues, both male and female, to clear her from the cloying aura of terror that persistently clung to her. Moreover, two of my friends were so alarmed by their contact with her, that they politely, but firmly, refused to help.

That aura that she carried with her was too strong to ignore!

I would never again allow myself, or my wife, to become involved with such a case, unless it concerned a member of my family, or a very close friend. I understand that Miss F has since died, at a respectable age, and I can only hope that her passing at the end was peaceful and untouched by such terror.

I am certain of one thing. Miss F had herself become involved with ritual-magic, as part of a group or coven dedicated to the magical pursuit of temporal power. In other words, she had become enmeshed in the practice of what is commonly known as Black Magic. Her methods of defence against psychic attack indicated that.

Exorcism by a properly ordained priest, rabbi, imam, clergyman, or minister is only used as a last resort in the battle against evil, and it is by no means always successful. It is usually practised in order to expel a possessing entity, or even entities, which, apparently, have taken over control of the body of some unfortunate person.

I certainly witnessed something very similar to possession, when I was a sixteen-year-old boy. It was in the case of a family friend, a young doctor, who had become unable to control an experiment that he had initiated. This intelligent and sensitive physician had spent time in India, during the early thirties, and had recently retired from service with the Indian army.

A Scot by origin, he was a deep-thinking and caring person, married only a year before to a lovely girl, who was now pregnant. She was also deeply worried about her husband's health, in view of the strange things that were happening to him.

Doctor J would wake up in the night with his hands working uncontrollably, the tips of his fingers touching and jerking back and forth, while signalling a kind of code. This was as a result of an experiment which the young doctor had devised, in order to synthesize a contact with an external entity, only, in Doctor J's case, as an experienced physician, he believed that the actual link he had established was with his own unconscious mind.

At least, that is how he had rationalized the experiment.

He had been led into this area of the behaviour of the human mind through the phenomena he had witnessed, while practising medicine on the Indian sub-continent.

Doctor J had used his hands as the method of communication, sitting with them held in front of him, with the fingertips touching and allowing his wrists full play, so that his hands could rock backwards or forwards to spell out a simple code.

If I remember correctly, the vowels were denoted by the number of times his hands jerked backwards, once for A, twice for E, etc., while the consonants were indicated by the opposite process, the hands moving *forwards*, in the same way, so that, for instance, B was once, C was twice and so on.

The object of this method was to ensure that no intermediate system, such as our Victorian table, was used in these experiments in communication, only a part of the communicator's body being directly employed to receive the code.

The experiment had been successful in that, by this odd method, a number of messages had been received and, even when difficult questions had been asked by Doctor J, the answers to which were unknown to him, the encoded replies had proved later to be a hundred per cent correct!

Unfortunately, the experiment had become uncontrollable and he would wake up in the night with his fingers in the transmitting position and his hands wildly rocking out the code.

Although the manifesting entity, who claimed to be a Hindustani, was not evil, Doctor J still could not rid himself of its possessive influence. Eventually, he had come to see Pop, more in despair than with much hope of being helped.

This sensible and practical physician knew a considerable amount about psychiatry, and he had already exhausted the explanations offered by that form of therapy. My father was Doctor J's last chance. Otherwise, he felt that he would have to retire as a practising physician, for reasons of mental imbalance.

This would have been a great loss to medicine, as this skilled and caring physician had built up an excellent practice in Folkestone, and was the trusted attending doctor to many of our friends, as well as being our own family doctor.

After listening to the young doctor's story, my father decided to have a sitting with him in our own home, not with the intention of holding a rescue circle, but to allow him to manifest his strange condition among friends.

Present at this sitting were my mother and Doctor J's wife, my brother and, at my earnest request, for I liked the doctor a lot, myself.

I clearly remember that the sitting took place in full light, on a summer evening, probably at the weekend, after the doctor had finished his surgery and during my school holidays.

The circle started conventionally enough with a short prayer and a general air of relaxation, and it wasn't long before Doctor J started to manipulate his hands in that odd way.

As he did so, he spelled out the message in this strange code and soon the whole affair became almost hypnotic, as his hands moved faster and faster and the letters spilled from his lips in a rapid stream. All the time one of us was writing down the letters as they were spelled out, but it was difficult to keep up with the very rapid movement of Doctor J's hands.

The replies coming from him were in response to questions which my father was putting to the manifesting entity. These were in English, but were apparently understood by the entity controlling the doctor's hands, presumably because they were being re-transmitted to the manifesting entity in the form of ideas in Hindustani, through the doctor's unconscious mind.

The entity claimed to be an Indian, a professional wrestler who had died through injuries, received during a fight.

At this point in the sitting my father decided to put Doctor J into a light trance, and soon the young physician relaxed into a deep sleep. His breathing became slower and more deliberate, and he appeared to pass into a deeper state of trance.

In reply to my father's questions, a different voice now issued from Doctor J's mouth, speaking in a guttural language and obviously in a state of distress. It was almost as if the entity was urgently trying to convey the essence of the story, which he had previously transmitted in code, using the doctor's hands.

His replies in that strange guttural voice were of course completely incomprehensible to us, so the entity, who was now apparently in complete control of the doctor's body and obviously deeply distressed, suddenly stood up and proceeded to act out a kind of weird charade, as though he was wrestling.

I shall never forget the feeling of tension as the doctor, now crouched in a wrestler's stance, circled an imaginary opponent, at times seeming to reach out to get a grip on his invisible adversary, while constantly moving with the balance, grace and speed of a trained athlete.

Suddenly it seemed to us, as the spellbound watchers, that he became locked in his unseen opponent's grip and, before our astonished eyes, Doctor J's body was lifted clear off the ground and bent savagely backwards, his spine twisted horribly and unnaturally. In a continuation of the same movement, he was flung down on to the carpet, landing heavily and in such a way as to convey the ghastly impression that his back had been broken.

At the same time, a horrifying scream ripped out from his throat, indicating that this was the moment of the agonizing death that the entity had suffered.

It was really terrifying!

Understandably, his wife fainted.

While my mother comforted the young mother-to-be, Pop and my brother tended to Doctor J, helping him up from the floor where he had been lying in that shockingly unnatural position, and sitting him confused but otherwise, amazingly, untouched by his extraordinary experience.

What is more, the doctor suffered no subsequent ill-effects whatsoever from that extraordinary charade, though we all would have sworn that, at one moment, his back had apparently been dislocated, or even broken.

I have described his whole case more fully in *The Door Marked Summer*, but I have kept this version as brief as possible to illustrate the type of extraordinary phenomena I witnessed in my youth.

We, as a family, lost touch with Doctor J and his wife during the war and I only met him, for a brief moment, at a meeting of the Freedom Association nearly forty years later.

I recognized him immediately, but then how could I ever forget him?

During the course of my life I have known some of the top European mediums and psychics and some of these made their way to America, where I met them again. Many of them told me, and I believe them because I knew them well and they had earned my trust, that they had been consulted by politicians and businessmen and women, in the highest positions in their countries.

They never volunteered their clients' names, because all of them practised their art with the strictest professional ethics, like priests at the confessional, or physicians with their patients, and of course I never asked for that sort of detail.

But it has struck me forcibly that there are a lot of top politicians and directors of industry in many countries, who put their faith in such guidance through mediums and psychics, yet who openly condemn these same practices, or at least never let it be known that such consultations have been sought by them, personally.

Nevertheless, it has become obvious to me that a significant amount of the world's affairs are being guided by these methods, just as they were in ancient times, and that we, the people, who are deeply affected by such far-reaching political and economic decisions, should have the right, as we have elected these politicians, or invested in these huge business enterprises, to know if and when such mediums and psychics are being consulted.

However, no shrewd person in that situation is going to give such information to their constituents, or shareholders, but the least they can do is *not* to condemn the very practices that they employ in the course of their careers.

There are so many points that I want to make to try to convince people that there are other sources of guidance available to them, when all the normal ones have failed to alleviate their problems.

Prayer really is effective!

I assure you that these words are not easy to write, because anyone putting them down has the feeling that they are opening themselves to snide and vicious criticism, by those who know the least about such matters.

I am always ready to listen to *constructive* criticism, but I firmly close my mind to negative and destructive carping.

Nevertheless, I felt impelled to write this book, mainly based on my own experiences, in the hope that in some small way it may help to answer a few of the questions regarding the existence of paranormal powers in the human mind, and the animal mind as well, and perhaps throw a little more light on the relationship between all forms of life on our planet.

As I have pointed out, I am not a Guru, but I do believe that I am fortunate enough to have been shown, and even to have experienced a fraction of the paranormal phenomena, which most bigoted technologists so cavalierly reject, outright.

I have also been lucky enough to have met and count as my friends some outstanding scientists and philosophers, who have been witnesses to similar phenomena. I thank them all for their kindness in freely sharing with me their impressions and knowledge.

I have personally experienced and observed the effect of valid healing and I accept, unreservedly, that a genuine healer *can* affect other less fortunate people's lives by easing their suffering and trauma.

Furthermore, I believe that it is important that I should speak out against certain evil practices that have been and still are being carried out against the public, *especially* to the grave disadvantage of creative minds, who are often by their very nature innocent of deceit

254

and, therefore, are such easy targets for unscrupulous manipulators.

Imaginative and creative minds hold the keys to the welfare, health and happiness of the people of the world and therefore, I consider that such conscienceless plagiarists are the real enemies of the people.

At least let us hope that I have drawn these readers' attention to the sort of attempts at mind-manipulation, which constantly pressure his, or her, life.

Let me repeat the words of the wise person, who said: 'Eternal Vigilance is the price of Liberty.'

May God bless us all, with understanding, humility, and knowledge, and above all else, with the love of our fellow-beings on this earth.

The only advice I can give the reader is to question everything.

Listen to your Intuition and then filter it through your Rationale. If you do that, as my father often told me: 'You won't go far wrong!'

A SELECTED OF OTHER FINE TITLES
AVAILABLE FROM CORGI BOOKS